GLIMPSES

IOWA'S RURAL LEGACY

Recollections and Commentary

Published by the Iowa Farm Business Association Foundation

Note for Librarians: a cataloguing record for this book that includes
Dewey Decimal Classification and US Library of Congress numbers is
available from the National Library of Canada. The complete cataloguing
record can be obtained from the National Library's online database at:
www.nlc-bnc.ca/amicus/index-e.html
ISBN 1-4120-4350-6
Printed in Victoria, BC, Canada

TRAFFORD

Offices in Canada, USA, Ireland, UK and Spain
This book was published *on-demand* in cooperation with Trafford
Publishing. On-demand publishing is a unique process and service of
making a book available for retail sale to the public taking advantage
of on-demand manufacturing and Internet marketing. On-demand
publishing includes promotions, retail sales, manufacturing, order
fulfilment, accounting and collecting
royalties on behalf of the author.
Book sales in Europe:
Trafford Publishing (UK) Ltd., Enterprise House, Wistaston Road
Business Centre, Wistaston Road, Crewe CW2 7RP UNITED KINGDOM
phone 01270 251 396 (local rate 0845 230 9601)
facsimile 01270 254 983; info.uk@trafford.com
Book sales for North America and international:
Trafford Publishing, 6E–2333 Government St.,
Victoria, BC V8T 4P4 CANADA
phone 250 383 6864 (toll-free 1 888 232 4444)
fax 250 383 6804; email to bookstore@trafford.com

www.trafford.com/robots/04-2158.html

10 9 8 7 6 5 4 3 2

Table of Contents

Acknowledgements

The Farm Business Association Foundation is appreciative of the effort put forth by all the authors who submitted stories about their rural legacies for the book. The book itself is one that each of us will want to share with our grandchildren, great-grandchildren and hopefully, even their offspring. Change is ongoing, and it's important that we keep some perspective about the past and how it relates to today and to the future.

One of the authors, LaVern Patterson, was a close friend of mine and grew up just one mile east of my parents' farm near Essex, Iowa. My Dad was LaVern's 4-H Leader. LaVern was diagnosed with cancer in 2003. I asked LaVern to write a story for the book. Time went on and on, and I didn't get one. I sent him a very nice reminder and eventually got a phone call from his wife, Karen, asking if it was too late to submit a story. She was calling from the Red Oak, Iowa, hospital. LaVern had taken a turn for the worse. I told her that there was time! They worked on it and sent it off. About three weeks later, LaVern died. It is important to note his commitment to the book and to me. He said he would do it, and by golly, he did. Thank you, LaVern – job well done!!!

The Farm Business Association Foundation is in its "infancy" stage of life. It has accomplished some important projects, but the publishing of this book is one of the most significant ones. Without the help of our editors, Helen Randall and Aaron Qualio, and the cover and divider page design work of Mindy Samuelson, the book would not have materialized. In spring 2003, Jacqui Becker Fatka used the idea of this book for her project in an advanced journalism course at Iowa State University. We have received much insight from her work.

The profit from the sale of the book will be returned to rural Iowa. Rural Iowa is changing and will continue to do so. Our mission within the Farm Business Association Foundation is to be able to help/assist farm families, rural non-farm families and rural communities deal with the many changes, opportunities and decisions they face in the future. We certainly do not tell them what to do, but simply help them as they make their decisions to carry out their goals.

We had 70-plus articles submitted for the book. We were not able to use all of them. It was tough to decide what to use or not use. Every story submitted was very, very good. The Foundation hopes to publish a second edition in the future. Some of the articles not used in this edition will then be used in the next one. If you have a special story about your rural past, please share it with us.

Thank you,

Jim Almquist
President, FBAF

Introduction

By Neil Harl

The editors of "Glimpses: Iowa's Rural Legacy" took seriously the oft-quoted dictum that a good writer knows how to evoke the emotions. The assembled stable of writers has produced an interesting, highly readable–and nostalgic–volume. Some of the essays will make you laugh; some may bring tears to your eyes. But any one is worth the price of the book.

The era spanned by the essays represents perhaps the greatest period of change ever experienced by the agricultural sector since the dawn of civilization. The authors pick up the story in the early decades of the 20th century and carry the theme well past the mid-century, even into today.

As one pulls back from the details of how individuals and families coped with change as they continued the age-old task of providing food for an always-hungry world, the larger picture reveals two persistent forces that were impacting agriculture: (1) the enormous change in genetics and (2) the highly important technology of power. These two forces combined to assure that a growing population in the country would have an adequate food supply with a growing slice of production moved into export.

Just a brief personal note about each of those enormously important developments:

- In early February of 1937, my father, a tenant farmer in southern Iowa, issued marching orders to his second oldest son–"butt and tip every ear in the small crib." The year 1936 had been terribly dry (and hot), corn yields were down and the ears were small. But I did as I was told. My dad ran the ears through a hand corn sheller and that was the seed supply for the 1937 crop. The yields were better than in 1936–about 40 bushels per acre. But a few of the neighbors were using hybrid corn (too expensive, I can still hear my dad say). But he became a believer with the better yields, so in 1938, it was all hybrids–and the yields jumped to 60 bushels per acre. Sixty-five years later, just a short distance from where I sat in February of 1937, the yields hit 200 bushels per acre. That's an astounding increase in productivity. That phenomenon has boosted output, pressured prices and delivered the benefits mostly to consumers in the form of lower and lower food costs.

- The other earth-shaking development was the technology of power. My dad farmed with horses until the autumn of 1946. That's when the new John Deere B arrived at the local dealership, capping a two-year wait as the manufacturers ramped up peace-time production after throwing all of their capacity into the war effort. A Model B, identical to Dad's 1946 tractor, now sits in our machinery storage shed in a tiny corner, alongside our tenant's behemoths, with more than 10 times the power of that Model B. Still, it requires just one person to navigate the behemoths, the same as was needed for the Model B and the same as was required for a four-horse hitch from decades back. The substitution of capital for labor has been truly awesome.

And we wonder why agriculture has changed so much! The consequences are felt in every small town in the country and in every family involved in food production. Nostalgia aside, there's little chance of a reversal.

That's the compelling reason why it's so important for those who didn't live through that period of such great change to learn of the day-to-day experiences. That's if we care about preserving for future generations a sense of what life was like in mid-20th century rural America. Those who have worked on this modest volume obviously do care. In every essay, you can sense the economic pressures, the richness of the social fabric and the enduring optimism of farm families, even in the face of adversity.

The over-arching features of the period of great change were the Great Depression and World War II. The Great Depression will be memorialized in history as the time of unprecedented low prices for commodities in real terms and the unprecedented shift in farm policy that shaped demand and supply for the rest of the century. The Great Depression also figures prominently in instilling in the young people in the generations that lived through it that whatever they were going to have at life's end, it was unlikely to come through inheritance. That spawned an economic groundswell of striving, hard-working survivors of that difficult period who contributed to the better times to come. World War II figures prominently in the picture not only for the economic contributions of the agricultural sector to the war effort, but also for helping to lift the sector economically to new levels of productivity in the post-war years.

Time has a way of flying by on winged feet. Almost in a blink of an eye, the agricultural world has changed. In a few short decades, few will be around to chronicle farm life in the early to mid-20th century. That's the contribution of the essays gathered here. Save this volume for your grandchildren and great-grand-children and file it away for generations beyond. For many of us, it was a defining period in our lives and one that deserves to be shared with our successors. For those who read these pages a century from now, it may seem a bit quaint and difficult to comprehend, but the experience will almost certainly enrich their lives.

Editor's Note: Neil E. Harl is a Charles F. Curtiss Distinguished Professor in Agriculture and Emeritus Professor of Economics at Iowa State University, Ames.

Living, Working & Learning

Maple Grove – A Rural Neighborhood

By Jack Van Laar

Growing up on a southern Iowa farm in the 1950s and 1960s provided me with unique experiences of rural life. Some of these experiences revolved around rural institutions and traditions quite common to my and previous generations, but essentially lost to following ones.

The sense of local farm community which formed the core of farm life is what I refer to as the rural neighborhood. For many, the term neighborhood evokes thoughts of families living within a few blocks of each other or on a common street in a town, city or suburb. But when I was growing up, there were definitely rural farm neighborhoods; mine even had a name, the Maple Grove Community. Maple Grove consisted of several family farms dotting an area of Grand River bottomland and the ridges surrounding the river valley. This was neither the name of our

township nor that of the nearest town, but it provided identity to our own special rural neighborhood.

The neighborhood farmers, baby boomers of the post-WWI era, inherited many values and perceptions from their parents who were products of the Great Depression. They were raising their own families in the post-WWII era at a very productive and prosperous time for agriculture. They were a vigorous, industrious group, making the most of new, more-powerful machinery in concert with much hard labor, which was shared throughout the neighborhood. They were producing for a growing market and were a rather homogenous group, having very similar farm sizes (usually 80-160 acres) and enterprises; you could describe one family farm and be fairly close to describing every family farm in the neighborhood.

Typical crop rotations included equal proportions of small grains and hay to the corn and soybeans. They had all mixes of livestock with moderate herd and flock sizes. Several farm families had a few dairy cows to nurse orphan calves, supply milk for the home table and provide cream to sell in town to supplement the household account. My mother always kept a few dozen hens as well for this purpose. Even after the small local egg and cream produce stations closed, she continued for many years to sell a few dozen eggs each week to townspeople desiring farm fresh eggs. The farm neighborhood was indeed a collection of very diversified, but similar, moderately prosperous and thrifty family farm units.

The earliest formal institutions I recall at the center of our farm neighborhood were a country school and church. For kindergarten, I was in the one-room country school house. The school house was a stucco structure with a diamond-shaped white wooden plaque centered above the front door; it was aptly named the Diamond School. There were only three students in my class, but we shared the room with about 20 others comprising all the other elementary and middle school grades. That was the final year classes were held there, but I will always have vivid memories of that unique open learning environment. The next year, all classes were moved to town, about four miles away. Within a few short years, that district merged with one in a neighboring town. Though even that district no longer exists, the Diamond School still stands. For many years after its closing, it remained a center of social activity for the Maple Grove community, giving service to numerous Christmas celebrations, bridal and baby showers, box and pie suppers and other social events. These activities were planned and managed by a neighborhood group known as the Maple Grove Boosters. I have few recollections of the church across the road, except for vague memories of a school Christmas program I participated in. Consolidation claimed this church as well, and the structure was removed long ago.

There is something lost in the passing of rural neighborhoods such as Maple Grove. I don't suggest that we reinstate the model as it existed, but many of the features of farming and society in general which made it work so well then are non-existent or have changed greatly since. However, the concept of building a sense of rural neighborhood is as important now as it was then. Rural dwellers today are a very diverse group, with wide differences in lifestyles, goals and plans for land use and rural dwelling. These differing views quite often come into conflict. For all their connectedness with the world via technology, rural dwellers today tend to be more isolated than ever from their own neighbors.

Although more challenging today, it is perhaps more critical that such neighborly networks be established. It all starts with people making an effort to be good neighbors themselves. Dr. Paul Lasley, Rural Sociologist at Iowa State University points out the importance of good neighboring skills regarding community health and quality of life. He contends that these are somehow slipping in both rural and urban areas today. Neighborliness involves some time spent in communication with each other to better understand each others' needs and aspirations. This communication can help to establish common ground and work through possible areas of conflict. It is only when people know each other that they can begin to trust each other and, as a result, work together towards community improvements. From neighboring and cooperation can arise mutual arrangements between neighbors to work for the common good of the neighborhood. Perhaps contemporary versions similar to our old Maple Grove Boosters will be reborn across the rural landscape someday and help restore the rural neighborhood community pride and oneness that I knew in my childhood.

Threshing in the Mid-1940s

By Rita Collier Dvorak

Threshing time was an exciting time for a farm kid. For those doing the work however, it represented seemingly endless hours in the hot sun, straw and chaff. It usually took place during July.

The threshing operation took many hands, so farmers in the neighborhood got together to form what was called a threshing ring. My father owned the machine in our ring. Several farmers and some hired help would constitute a crew of 10 to 15 men. They went from one farm to another, depending on whose crop was ready first. Each farmer provided fuel for the tractor that provided power for the threshing machine. A pulley on the tractor was connected by a long belt to a pulley on the machine. That farmer also provided his horses and equipment, and food for the workers. Other neighbors furnished horses and wagons, somehow trading around until things came out even.

The farmer's wife provided dinner (at NOON!) and lunch at mid-afternoon. Other wives of the crew would come to help if needed. The activity that transpired in the kitchen is another whole story.

The bundles of straw and oats, previously shocked, were now ready to be picked up. There were usually two teams of horses and wagons; four men would go with each wagon–one to drive the team, two to throw bundles on the wagon and one to stack them. Once full, the wagon went from the field to the yard where the straw stack would be made. The men then threw the bundles into the threshing machine which separated the oats and straw. The oats moved up an inside elevator and through a pipe into a wagon. When the wagon was full, another man hauled the oats to the granary.

This wooden building had several "rooms," or bins to hold oats, soybeans or shelled corn in storage for the livestock. It was important that the grain be dry enough to keep all winter, or it would spoil. Two men would scoop the oats into the bin, then return the wagon to the threshing machine for another load.

Meanwhile, the straw that had been separated from the oats went up a long pipe which could be adjusted upward as the straw stack grew. One man was the stacker, in charge of shaping and packing the straw so the stack would hold a rounded, firm shape which helped to shed the rain–this preserved the quality of the straw, which was used for bedding for the cattle and hogs. Usually, the stacker was the farmer who used it. Making a good stack, with just a pitchfork and one's feet was an art that the farmer took much pride in. Stacking was the hottest, dirtiest job. Dad's overalls and shirt would be totally soaked with sweat and his face and neck full of chaff in spite of his broad-brimmed straw hat.

I remember two times during threshing when Dad had heat stroke and had to be taken to a nearby hydrant where he lay in the shade and was given small amounts of water at a time while being fanned with several straw hats. I was a very frightened 6-or-7-year-old then, knowing that the situation could be serious–people were known to die from heat stroke if they didn't receive proper attention. The men always had buckets of drinking water available in the field and near the threshing operation. Replacing the water was my job, and on hot days, they drank lots of water!

Each threshing job took from one to three days or sometimes longer if it rained, setting back the work. The crews started mid-morning (after chores were done and the "dew was off") and quit in time to do the milking and nighttime chores like making sure the horses were properly cared for; supper was after dark.

It was a time for rejoicing when all the threshing jobs were completed, with the oats and straw safely stored. Then, normal summer work could continue and maybe, if things worked out, the family had time for a short vacation or time to go visit "far away" relatives across the state. When we returned, it was time to put up sweet corn and go to the county fair. If we were lucky, we might even go to the Iowa State Fair for a couple of days!

These memories are indelible for me. I hope that future generations may have a glimpse into the past (even though it was only 60 years ago!) and have an appreciation for the physical work, the teamwork and for being close to the earth. May they take pride in their heritage in rural Iowa!

First Tractor Cab

By Virgil Lemke

As tractors became more popular and necessary, farmers soon found that they were very cold to ride in the fall and early spring. The so-called "heat houser" became the necessary addition and did provide warmth when going against the wind. However, when the wind was blowing from the back, all the heat blew ahead, making it very cold for the operator once again. It was hard to dress for comfort with these conditions; too cold going one way, too hot going the other. Because of this, we had to put on a lot of bulky clothes making movement difficult.

Some county graders and road equipment were starting to add a little more protection, but it hadn't been offered on the market for farm tractors yet. One real windy, cold, fall day, I rode with our township road maintainer to see just how well a windbreak of glass would do; I found it unbelievable. That cold, sharp wind was no problem regardless of our direction. Instantly the wheels in my head started turning, and I began to ask the operator questions about operating the machine from inside his little hut. I thanked him for the ride and advice, and walked home a lot faster than normal because I didn't want to forget all the information I was given. I was going to convince Dad and Mom of the idea I had come up with.

I wanted to build a little hut on top of our tractor to help keep whoever was driving it warm. At first, Mom and Dad thought it wasn't worth all the extra work it would take. Also, they were wondering what all the neighbors would think of such a thing running around on the Lemke farm; this was the main topic of conversation for the next week. Little by little, I noticed that no one was really against the idea, just suspicious of whether or not it would actually work and, of course, what it would cost.

There was an old brooder house behind the grove in which

Mom raised leghorn roosters for butchering. One night during a wind storm, it blew over and broke all to pieces. I asked if I could salvage some material from it for my hut; I got the go-ahead because they wanted it cleaned up anyway. My idea was now beginning to take shape.

There were two six-light windows in the brooder house that hadn't been broken. I decided that they would work well for side vision. There was also an old, unused 4-foot-square storm window in the basement of our house that would be just right for the front. I saved all the boards from the brooder house that weren't rotten; most of the 2x4s were okay. I then drove our old Oliver "70" into the corn crib alley, and started building.

My hut actually went together pretty well, until I needed some boards sawed in a circular line to fit the curvature of the tractor frame. Dad came and looked in on me occasionally. One time, he said to leave the hard to fix areas open, and let the heat houser from the tractor motor cover them. Now I'll admit, I had not thought of that; I had not figured on using the heat from the tractor motor, but it sounded right. It didn't take very long to get the hut all framed up, put the windows in place or nail the roof down solid. Mom even got interested and came out to look; she thought that I should put an old quilt or curtain in the back to help hold the heat in. The problem with that was that I had to be able to reach and move the plow levers while plowing. We just decided to wait and see how everything else worked and add the back part later. One warm day, the hut even got a fresh paint job; it was a green tractor, but our new addition was red, which matched the wheels nicely.

The hut was barely completed before we started picking the corn. I hadn't told Uncle Elmer about this idea, but I knew his comments would be favorable. He really looked it over when he first saw it, so I told him to try it out. I told him to drive down the road a mile to see how it felt before we hooked it on to the corn picker. Away he went in road gear. By the time he returned, he had taken off his jacket and had the biggest smile on his face. The tractor's motor had warmed up, and all the heat came through the cab; he said it felt just like summer again.

As we began picking the corn, cars would drive by and almost come to a stop while observing our new hut. On days when snow squalls blew, I really waved at cars going by. For fun, I even rolled my shirt sleeves up one day.

Guys used to come out to our place from Des Moines to pheasant hunt, and they really appreciated the hut. They would walk awhile and after getting pretty tired, they'd climb on top of the hut for a ride. It was plenty strong to hold them. When coming to the end of a strip of standing corn, pheasants often would fly out, and hunters could get their limit easily.

As I wrote this story, my mind went back 40 years when Galen Jacobsen, my wife Ardis' brother, became a tractor casualty. He was not feeling the best, with a cold, and while driving the tractor, he apparently had a blackout and fell off. Had he been in a tractor cab and blacked out, he would not have fallen off, and would be alive today. He was in Europe for World War II and survived all those dangers, only to come home and be killed by a tractor. Tractor cabs provide a lot more comfort, but they also are able to save many lives.

Cigars Behind the Barn

Told By Carl Carlson to His Wife, Judy

For sixty years the pine lumber barn
had held cows, horses, hay, harness, tools, junk
amid the prairie winds...
And the barn was a witness, stood and saw it all.

From "The People, Yes," by Carl Sandburg

The barn on the farm of Orley Havens witnessed two young chaps smoking their first cigar; I was one of those chaps. The other guy was my friend, Bub. We were spending one of the last "dog days of summer" at our grandparents' farms located across the road from each other. Both of our mothers were at work in town, feeling assured that their 12-year-old sons were "out-of-trouble."

In 1945, when we were about to embark on our teen years,

the grown-up men we aspired to emulate smoked something. The one exception was my other grandfather, Rev. Carlson. He was a smoke-free gent.

Out at the farm, Grandpa Havens kept a wooden box of cigars for himself; he enjoyed one long cigar every night after supper. It must have seemed like a reward for a good day's work to lean back in his favorite chair and have one good smoke. His cigars had the appealing scent of fine quality. To me, his eldest grandson, it was the scent of successful manhood.

Bub and I had already tried smoking earlier that summer. We'd tried to smoke ripe sourdock seeds rolled up in toilet paper. A truly awful experience! There had to be something better to use for an experimental smoke. A good cigar seemed right.

It was easy to snitch a cigar from Grandpa's box kept on the shelf under the ashtray of his smoking stand. Grandma was resting upstairs after she'd finished the dinner dishes and Grandpa had gone back to mowing the final cutting of alfalfa hay. With the cigar tucked in the bib pocket of my overalls and a side-pocket full of stick matches, we strode across the barnyard like two farmers headed out to choose a new bull. Our stride was free of sheepishness that might reveal our mission to any unexpected adult surveillance. With a leap over the watering tank we arrived at our secluded spot in the shade behind the barn.

With only the barn as a witness, we unwrapped the cigar, cut it in half, lit it up and puffed away. I wonder now what we talked about at that moment. After we'd been there quite awhile something startled us, so we buried the cigar butts, using our boot heels to dig their grave in dry hoof powder and took off running toward the house. The escape route out of the cattle lot was the path by which we'd come. To escape, we had to jump up on the tank edge and run a few steps around the top to the other side of the fence. Let's just say that running and jumping at that time were too much for Bub's nauseous stomach resulting from inhaling some of the cigar smoke; he vomited as he leaped on the tank ledge. To cleanse his shame, he dunked his head under the water tank's slimy green water, which was not something wise to do in the heat of summer when the tank water was stale. Icky! He swished the green moss off his nose and spit out the stagnant gulp.

I was lucky, I hadn't gotten sick, so I could immediately tease him for his wimpy ways. Put down by my mockery and not wanting to appear inferior he retorted, "But I got the butt end and that is the strongest!" Bub was a competitive guy who preferred to "end up on top." It was that quickness of mind and body that earned him a quarterback position on our high school football teams. He also went on to play varsity football for four years at Iowa State Teacher's College.

It had been half a century since I'd recalled that smoking event. It had rapidly flashed back to my mind when I first viewed a new watercolor painting of that old Haven's barn with a cement tank beside it. The granddaughter of the next-door farmer, Kay Kapfer Wall of Ames, painted that watercolor of Grandpa Haven's barn for us. She'd used new photos of the barn, in dilapidated condition, and our collective memories as her visual guide. While tramping through head-high weeds to take those photos, we'd tripped over half-buried chunks of the tank, laying like a broken, big flower pot for trashy Chinese Elm trees.

Change & Transition:
The Mechanical Revolution

By Lynn Benson

Raised the oldest son of a third generation Iowa farmer and his school teacher wife, I have always been proud of my small town, rural American upbringing. I was born in 1939 and thus lived through one of the greatest transitions in American agriculture.

Our family's farm near Sidney was purchased by my great grandfather G.S. Benson in 1881. Gaylord was born and educated in New York and originally settled in Hamburg, Iowa, where he taught school and owned a soap factory. The farm provided a comfortable living to two generations of Bensons, but by the time my father took over the farm operations after his father's death in a tragic farm accident in the late 1920s, life in small town, rural America was beginning to change.

Education was always important in our family. Four of the six children in my father's family went to college; two of these four were girls, which was rare in the early 1900s. My father also had planned to go to college to be a teacher and a coach, but those plans changed with the early death of his father.

My father began farming before the great mechanical revolution in American agriculture. Horsepower of that day was truly "horse" power and my father's early farming was done in much the same way as by his father and grandfather. It was hard, physical work. Eventually, machine power began to take over. My father purchased his first tractor in the year of my birth and always took great pride in the fact that it was the first Ford Ferguson tractor in his local community. From then on, farm life as my parents and grandparents knew it, was to change rapidly and forever.

Despite being born during this time of great change and transition, I've always felt fortunate to have experienced life on a small, family farm in a small, rural Iowa community. As a youngster, I was more of an observer than a participant in the "old way," but I shall always be grateful for the experience. My children and grandchildren can only read about it; it's not the same.

While the mechanical revolution had begun, we still had several horses and still did a lot of work ourselves. I often used horses to carry cold water in a jug (wrapped in wet burlap that hung over the saddle horn) to the men in the hayfield. I drove the horse that pulled the hay fork from the hayrack into the barn. I rode and operated the oat binder (now pulled by the Ford tractor and driven by my father), and I shocked the oat bundles so they could cure before the thresher came by our neighborhood. I helped Dad butcher hogs and grandmother dress chickens. I milked cows by hand and cranked the cream separator; the latter I couldn't wait to do, but soon wished I had.

One of the real losses to the mechanical revolution was the "neighboring" that went on in several of the family operations. In our neighborhood, about six families would work together when it came threshing or haying time. I first remember putting up "loose" hay pitched on the hay wagons by hand. In later years, however, balers did the work and the young boys of the neighborhood threw the bales on the wagon. Dad, now graduated to driving the tractor, drove slowly down the rows of baled hay. The food prepared by my mother for these crews was such a treat; our friends always liked to work on the "haying crew" because of Mom's cooking. It was hard work, but we felt pride in a job well done, of working together to help each other, of community and being good neighbors. All these were good life lessons that sadly, are now gone for much of rural America.

Another now-extinct social experience was small town, rural Iowa on a Saturday night. It was before the days of television, mass communication, shopping centers, computers and even electricity in some parts of rural Iowa. Before all of those "improvements," Saturday night in Sidney, as in most rural towns, was a great social occasion.

Sidney had four grocery stores, three barbers, four automobile dealers, five gasoline stations, two clothing stores, two furniture stores, two doctors, two dentists, four churches...need I go on? Following the band concert on the Courthouse lawn, Mom and Dad would sell their eggs and cream. Mom would then go to the grocery store to buy the week's supply of food, and Dad would go to the barbershop for his weekly trim. After that, Dad and Mom would visit with friends and neighbors until we kids got out of the movie theater (yes, we even had one of those). In fact, we got our weekly dose of world news on the "newsreels" before the feature film. I suppose none of us would like to return to those "good old days," but "neighboring" and "Saturday night in town" are two fond memories of my growing up in rural Iowa. Their demise, in my opinion, was a real loss to our way of life.

Education was always stressed in our families, and my wife, Marilyn, and I both went to Iowa State University and found careers off the farm in agriculture and education. We still own and live on the family farm. Our children and their families, now scattered across the country, still consider this home and like to return frequently to their roots.

Life in small town, rural Iowa has been good to us and to our families. We feel grateful and truly blessed.

The Barn

By Jim Almquist

In the summer of 2003, I finally got the barn my Dad built torn down. I intended to tear it down two years ago. I had planned to have the Essex Fire Department do it, so I went to the Essex City Hall to find the Fire Chief. While there, I ran into my cousin Wayne. I told him, "I'm making arrangements to burn the barn down." He said, "Oh Jim, do you know that your Dad built that barn?" That comment stifled my plans for a while. Finally, I decided to proceed, but not without much thought and many memories.

The barn was built in late 1943 after our farm was hit by a massive tornado in the spring of '43. Everything but the house and milk shed was destroyed. The milk shed was located 30 feet north of the house with a hand pump/well in between the two buildings. The torna-do pulled the pump out of the well and laid it out on the ground just as though you had done it by hand. We found my 4-H dairy heifer (Judy) standing in a stock tank full of water! Not injured, just con-fused. Basically every window in the house was broken; glass was even imbedded in the piano. The tornado killed only one ani-

mal, a diary cow (Roany), hit on her back by the falling cupola. The storm carried lumber, full of nails, all over the farm, as the cows grazed in the pasture, they'd consume nails, which eventually would kill them.

It was great that neighbors pitched in and helped with the clean up. We removed nails from the boards–all the boards. We used very little of the old lumber for the new barn. For now, however, we had no barn in which to milk the cows. The tornado left an implement storage shed, so Dad took the implements out and converted it to a milking shed. No electricity, dirt floor and open to the south; quite a mess when it rained. It seemed every time it rained, the wind was from the south and the floor/dirt got very wet. It wasn't fun for us or the cows. We survived until the new barn was finished. We were in before winter!

We always had a number of cats on the farm, and they enjoyed it when I milked the cows. Occasionally, when bored, I would squirt milk into the mouths of the cats as I milked. Those cats were very acrobatic and could get that stream of milk at almost any angle. The Surge milker my Dad bought to replace our having to hand-milk was great. I doubt the cows appreciated it, however, since we had to hang the milker over their backs with a strap and attach the milker to the teats while standing on our head. But it saved a lot of time and worked well. The cats didn't like it either, but they survived. I will always remember opening up the barn door in the wintertime with all the cows in there. That warm air and manure smell would hit you right in the face! I think that is why we always had breakfast after we had finished milking.

I was very active in 4-H, as was my Dad. I have always said that the two best 4-H leaders I have ever been associated with were my Dad and my wife, Anne. I had a bunch of 4-H projects–dairy heifers, beef heifers and steers. When we would take off for the Page County Fair, it would take a very large truck to haul everything. It seemed that every time I would show my dairy or beef heifers, one or two would be in heat. That means they'd climb on the heifer's back in front of them in the show ring. It was very embarrassing.

After I graduated from Essex High School, Dad decided that milking was not profitable and "too damned much work." He sold the dairy cows and got Angus cows and started a beef cow herd! I asked myself, why didn't he do that when I was home? The barn was used for the Angus bull, farrowing house and calves. After the dairy cows were gone, it never was the same; it was just a building, and it started to go downhill. We did store hay in the hay mow. Originally, it was loose hay. Then we moved to bales of hay and straw. The barn, uniquely, had two storage areas—one to store ground corn for the dairy cows and one for grain such as oats. Speaking of oats, I hated scooping oats by hand into the grain bin. Not so much for the work, but the oat hulls made me itch. The more you'd sweat, the more you'd itch!

I finally got tired of seeing the barn slowly disintegrate and weeds grow up around it. It was depressing. I talked to my cousin, Tom, and asked him if he knew of someone who could tear the barn down. To make a long story short, a gentleman came in with his bulldozer, cut off the poles in the middle of the barn, dug a massive hole to the west of the barn and simply went inside with his dozer and pushed it into the hole. I was amazed! The next step was burning the lumber and then covering it up. Sadly, there now is no sign that a barn ever existed there. In the 2004 growing season, that spot was planted with corn. No longer will you see this big white barn sticking up over the hillside when you drive from Red Oak and come within 3 miles of Essex on Highway 48. It's sad; some will say its progress. It's change, not progress. The countryside is getting even more isolated and bare. Thank heavens I have some great pictures of the barn to remind me of all it represented.

William Secor Sr.

By Bill Secor

In 1946, I rented 320 acres of land in Webster County with my father. The landowners allowed me to rent additional land if I promised not to short-change their farm. I always farmed every acre as if I owned it. All livestock and crop work was done at the proper time and to the best of my ability. In 2000, I purchased the 320 acres on contract from the landowners' heirs.

In the early 1950s, I rented an additional 240 acres located about two miles from our home. However, when the owner's nephew came home from the service, the owner said that he felt that his nephew should get to farm that place. Though I was disappointed to give up renting that farm, I agreed with the owner and we remained friends. The nephew and I also became very good neighbors and friends. What that taught me, though, was to watch for other opportunities. One such opportunity arose in 1956 when I purchased my first farm, one mile to the north, for approximately $300 per acre. More opportunities for land ownership arose in the 1960s, and I purchased two additional 80-acre farms.

As my hair began to gray, I felt that landowners might decide to rent to younger men, so every time I could arrange down payment on a farm, I would buy it. In the late 1960s, I was renting another 160 acres from a woman that received that farm in a divorce settlement. She wanted to sell me 80 acres so she could buy a house in town. Later, she decided to sell the total farm but not the building site. I bought it on contract. I purchased another 80 acres, about five miles south and east of our home from a private owner financed by the Federal Land Bank.

In the late 1970s, I bought two additional farms. One was 80 acres, which needed tilling. The other was 112 acres with a large high line running through on the 80-acre line. Both of these farms were expensive, $2,800-plus.

Then the farm crisis of the1980s rolled around. Things changed. In spring of 1980, my wife, who did all book work, mentioned that she felt my banker wasn't being as honest as he might be, and I should watch him. I made light of that, because he was a personal friend and the president of the bank. In August of 1980, my wife of 34 years died suddenly of a cardiac arrest. According to my financial records, I had approximately $2 million net worth. A sudden drop in land and crop values along with high interest rates contributed to a tremendous financial loss for us. When everything was settled in 1988, my financial statements indicated I had a negative $573,000. About half was lost in land value, the rest in one way or another was gone, perhaps lost by my banker.

Lesson: Always watch yourself so you don't get snowed.

I signed the final settlement agreements when I was hospitalized in Rochester for esophageal cancer surgery. The lawyer sent my son up with legal papers to have them signed because they thought I wouldn't survive the surgery. I fooled everyone, and am maybe dull, but still alive. In the settlement, I had to sell some of the land. I also lost the basis on two farms because of some debt forgiveness.

After the whole ordeal of the 1980s was over, my biggest problem was to overcome my personal feelings of being a failure. I learned that I couldn't dwell on the past, but rather needed to find a new direction for my life and be open to new opportunities.

Perhaps I should give you some background on my childhood. I came out of a very poor family. My father was taken in by a land scam in Louisiana. That, along with the 1930s Depression, never allowed my folks to rebound financially. As a result, none of us six children inherited anything from my folks. However, we were instilled with their strong faith in God and the example they set by always being honest and fair with everyone.

In later years, each month, we six children put some money into funds to provide for the care of our folks. My older brother's wife did the bookkeeping and paid the bills and I provided the home for them.

In addition to the health issues I mentioned above, I've also experienced many other health-related crises. In 1942, my first wife died a little over a year after we were married. That same year, I nearly died from an infected gall bladder that was ready to rupture. In 1999, I had a severe, uncommon heart problem, which caused restriction of blood flow out of my heart to the rest of my body. I was set up for cardiac bypass surgery and was under anesthesia before the extent of the problem was known. My physician daughter who accompanied me to the surgery suite made the decision that they should proceed with valve replacement and surgery on the wall between the lower chambers of my heart. They thought that I wouldn't survive that one either, but here I am, still kicking.

My son, William Jr., came back from college in 1980 and wanted to farm. We have worked together in crops with the planting and harvesting, but we each have our own individual operation. We have shared machinery through the years although, during the first years, I owned most of the machinery. The last several years we have operated around 3,000 total acres. In 2004, I'm letting my son farm some of the land I've been farming because over 300 acres that he had farmed has been sold.

During the 1950s, when I needed guidance on farm operation, I joined the Farm Business Association and have continued to benefit from their services for over 50 years. I'd like to take this opportunity to thank the FBA for their expertise in assisting us in farm management through the highs and the lows for over 50 years.

Life hasn't always been easy for me, but if I hadn't allowed myself to put the past away, new doors wouldn't have opened and allowed me to proceed.

Lessons I Learned Growing Up on the Farm

By Robert Dunaway

To get the flame going in the tank heater, we used kerosene, corncobs and stick matches. Then, we'd pile in some wood and top it off with coal to get the heater hot enough to melt the ice so the dairy cows could drink.

Farm chores were always harder during the winter. But the freshness of the air and the crispness of the snow under your feet seemed to be enough reward to make it the best time of year in my mind.

Ours was a small farm. The main chore tools were grain shovels, wide manure forks and tin, 5-gallon buckets. In the late 1940s and early 1950s, we fed the hogs in troughs and the cattle in feed bunks, carrying the corn to them in those buckets and then evenly spreading the protein supplement on top.

Later, when I–the last of 4 children–went off to college and the cheap labor force was gone, the dairy cows went to market and self-feeders replaced the troughs and bunks. I didn't mind; I had learned many good lessons in that farmyard.

Among valuable lessons I learned:

- You don't open the box on the old binder that's been sitting in the weeds for years; there may be a nest of bees...
- You don't run uphill; downhill is faster–after you open that binder box...
- If you decide to ride a steer, you don't tie the rope around both you and the animal...
- You don't try to shoot wasps with a BB gun...
- You can't wait too long to "stick" a bloated cow (she died)...

- When driving steel posts with a post driver, you should never, ever let your finger slip onto the top of the post as the driver is coming down...
- Country doctors pulled smashed fingernails off with a tool that looked a lot like a pliers...
- Country doctors didn't use Novocain...
- Even though clover is really dusty to bale, chewing tobacco is not the way to keep your throat clear when you're 16 and never chewed before...
- The neighbor who gave you the chewing tobacco can load the bales on the rack while you drive...
- You can drive a tractor straight even though you can't stand up after swallowing too much tobacco juice...
- Mice will run up pant legs if you don't tie twine around them when shelling out the corn crib...
- You don't pee on ant mounds...
- Corncob fights are fun until you forget to duck and your mother asks you what caused that rash on your forehead...
- Mulberries should be washed before you eat them...
- You shouldn't try to crawl under an electric fence with baling wire folded up in your back pocket...
- When testing to see if the electric fence is working, you hand your 5-year-old brother the blade of grass and tell him to see if he can lay it on the wire and hold it there (thanks to my brother, Jim, for teaching me that one)...
- And the one we all were told: You don't put your tongue on the pump handle in the wintertime!

Pullet Hayride

By Judith Schomberg Carlson

As family farms specialized their animal agriculture, chickens were usually the first to go; that wasn't the case for us. From 1935 to 1957, our mothers each kept a flock of chickens until the farm partnership of Schomberg & Padgett was divided into two separate operations. After that, each family kept individual poultry enterprises until our mothers became full-time caregivers for our frail fathers. A generation later, the visiting grandchildren viewed chicken chore-time as something special.

During the Schomberg & Padgett years, my mother, Geraldine, raised the young chickens at our place, while my Aunt Louise tended the hens at the Padgett place. When the time came to move the 350 or so pullets the half-mile between farmsteads, chicken chore-time proved to be no small task.

During the January thaw, Mother would scrub the brooder house and begin to lovingly prepare it for the 350 or so fluffy yellow baby chicks that would soon arrive by mail from the Hyline hatchery in Marengo, Iowa.

When mid-summer rolled around, we would have a big family day; the backyard would be turned into a slaughter operation for killing, picking, singeing, cleaning and cooling-out the rooster carcasses to be frozen for eating. Before we had home deep freezers in our cellars, we'd have to take the dressed birds to Roman and Liebe in Muscatine for wrapping, freezing and storing. Extra dressed birds were sold to Richards' Meat Market.

With a nip of fall in the air and pullets laying eggs large enough to sell, the date would be set for the pullet hayride.

Part of what makes a family activity special is the ritual of preparation, and such a preparation ritual was carefully completed before the pullets could be moved to the hen-house. Our grandfather, Frederick Schomberg, built the henhouse from hollow clay tile when he and his wife, May, bought the farm in Concord Township in Louisa County. It was a four-room house with a gable roof.

Most of the prior year's layers were sold to Swift & Company in Muscatine or to neighbors. Occasionally, some were moved to a shack in the maple grove, so there would be eggs to sell until the pullets were in full production.

It was the job of the young boys on the farm to clean out the manure; I doubt that they enjoyed that much. The hen house, feeders and water buckets would get a good scrubbing with lye water, while the roosts were coated with antiseptic creosote to destroy any mites, lice and other pests. Electric timers to turn the lights on at dusk and off at dawn were checked out, and the feeders and waters were placed to reduce the nuisance factor of the natural bird behavior to scratch in feed and bath in drinking water. The feeders were filled with ground corn oats processed through a hammermill. If any commercial feed was purchased, it was a mash that came in flowered cloth bags saved for home sewing. Pans of oyster shell grit were put out for the hens to eat to strengthen their egg's shells. Finally, the 4 to 5-gallon waterers were filled with clean water.

The real fun came with the hayride. The kids got to stay up past "going to bed with the chickens." Communication was in charades, because noise sent the pullets into a frightful frenzy. After daylight faded and the pullets slept soundly with their heads tucked under their wings in the brooder house or high in the pine grove, the crew stealthily approached the orchard.

My mother entered the dark brooder house as a "thief in the night" to pick up the drowsy birds one-by-one. She'd hand them out the door to our father, Ted, who would start them along the conveyer of kids to Uncle John who would place the pullets into the wooden coups piled on the hayrack. When the coups were full, the kids would climb up onto them to hold as many pullets by one leg as their small hands could grasp. Dad would drive the small tractor hitched to the hayrack out of the orchard and onto the bumpy, half-mile road between the two farmsteads.

The unloading process reversed the process. Dad and Aunt Louise would do the seemingly painless beak trims so the hens would be less likely to injure each other. At least one more roundtrip was needed to complete the move.

The aerial act of the night would come when Dad and the three young boys would climb leaning wooden ladders to get to the errant pullets that had chosen to roost in the tall cedar grove; an act worth watching in the faint circle of light cast by a flashlight. The ground crew spotters were to report where any scared pullets ran to escape their human predators.

Homemade Soap

By Lillian Thiemann

Homemade soap was not invented by my mother or her mother. No one knows for sure when the first batch of soap was brewed, stirred and successfully used for laundry. As the story goes, the first soap suds occurred when a native of Gaul used a hair dressing made of goat oil and beech tree ashes. He got caught in a rain storm one day and for the first time, man saw soap suds!

Another legend has it that about 3,000 years ago on a hill in Rome, grease from sacrificial animals became mixed with the ashes from the altar fires. When the mixture ran downhill into the Tiber River, the washer women found their laundry chores much easier.

When man first started actually making soap, the necessary alkali came from potash made from leaching wood ashes. The first pioneers in America made soap by leaching wood ashes to get the alkali to mix with the fat that could be spared from cooking and left over from butchering.

My mother's soap came out in hard, white bars. She made it until Gold Dust, Oxydol and some bar soaps like Naptha were available. For Mother to make her kind of soap, she needed two cups of cold water, eight cups of melted lard, one-half cup of ammonia, one-fourth cup of borax and one can of lye. First, the grease was warmed and measured into an enamel pan (lye would have ruined an aluminum utensil). The lye was then dissolved into the water in a glass mixing bowl. The lye water was slowly poured into the grease and stirred constantly with a wooden spoon or paddle. She then added the ammonia and borax and stirred for at least 20 minutes or until the mixture started to thicken. It was then poured into a shallow enamel pan or pasteboard box to cure for at least two weeks before cutting into bars for the family wash and other cleaning jobs.

Water and Stones

By Lillian Thiemann

My mother always had a rain barrel at the corner of our house to catch rainwater to wash our hair and water her houseplants. A lot of farm houses had cisterns, so they had soft water without setting out a barrel.

For a couple of summers in the early 1930s, no rain fell in the Midwest for weeks and weeks. Our well was not as deep as our neighbors, and sometimes Dad would have to go to one of them and get a barrel or two for us to use and to water the livestock. He had a water sled made with boards nailed across wooden runners that held two barrels. He put Mother's old wash tub over one and nailed some boards together to put over the other ones so the water didn't slosh out. He'd hitch one horse to this outfit and haul the water back home.

We had another use or two for that water sled. Sometimes we would hitch our pony to it and a couple of us would have a ride. Water sleds were also called stone boats. I'm sure you have driven through rural areas and noticed piles of stones in the corners of fields. Most farmers hauled stones off their fields in the spring. It seemed like every year a few came to the surface; Dad said they were heaved to the surface of the fields by the frost in the spring. They had to be taken off before the fields could be worked and planted. For many years the piles grew. Now they are disappearing. Farmers are selling them to landscapers for use around homes and for fireplaces. When it comes to water and stones, there will always be a need for both of them.

Many wells dried up those summers and, as a result, a lot of livestock were sent to market long before they were ready. Year after year, Midwest farmers planted their crops and the rains finally did come. The wells filled up once more and crops and livestock again thrived and produced.

To avoid such a critical water shortage again, the government (about 1937) began subsidizing the digging of farm ponds for those who had a lot of cattle. Deeper wells were also dug, tapping generous underground water sources. Soon, the Rural Electric Cooperative came through our area bringing electricity to pump the water. From then on, the rain barrel, the water sled and many of the windmills disappeared from the rural scene.

Wash Day

By Lillian Thiemann

Wash day at our house meant a lot of work. It took a lot of clothes for the six of us. The water pump, at the windmill, was about 40 feet from the house, half-way out to the barn. Each Monday morning, before he went out to milk the cows, Dad would carry enough water to the house to fill the old, dented copper boiler.

Today we still have one of those copper boilers, all shined up, sitting by the fireplace filled with wood. All I need to do is look at that thing, and it brings back memories of all the hard work a boiler meant to my mother; not only on wash day, but on canning days, too.

Mother would set the boiler on the cook stove, and Dad would fill it from the well. We had an old Majestic cook stove that swallowed up all the sticks and cobs we kids could gather the night before. By the time breakfast was over, dishes done and chickens fed, the water would be boiling. Mother always put some Lewis lye in the water to "break" it because it was so hard you couldn't get any suds no matter how much soap you put in. Once she added that lye, curds came to the top, and she skimmed them off (minerals in the water made it hard). She also always made

her own soap. She would shave that hard white soap into the water with a cabbage slicer—the kind used to make sauerkraut.

Part of the water would then be put in the wooden washing machine. In this, Mother washed the table cloths, dish towels, pillow slips, sheets and other less-soiled white things. She put the hand towels, socks, and men's underwear in the boiler first and later washed them in the machine.

The wooden washer had a stick handle that we kids had to push back and forth to turn the dolly inside the machine. The dolly "slushed" the clothes up and down. It must have been an awful job for Mother when we were all in school. Years later, Dad hooked it up to a gas engine. This made it easier, but then the only time Mother could wash was when Dad was around because she couldn't start the engine.

While we pushed back and forth, quarreling about who was working the hardest and pushing the longest, Mother carried more water in to rinse the clothes. She put a little bluing in the cold water to make the white things whiter and colored things brighter. After she got them all rinsed, we'd help her carry them out to the clotheslines at the back of the house. She hung them up herself, however. To her there was just one right way to hang out a wash and that was the way she did it; even in the winter, she hung them out. I can still see those sheet blankets and long johns, stiff as boards when they froze – and the long johns looking like they had ghosts in them!

Depression Era Technology

By Robert B. Hegland

I grew up on a rented 160-acre farm near Radcliffe, Iowa, during the 1930s. We didn't have electricity or running water in the house. On hot, windy days, my mother couldn't open the windows because of the dust; she had to put wet rags in the window sills to keep out the dust. Many nights we slept on the living room carpet because the upstairs was too hot; there was no insulation in those days!

In the winter, we had a cook stove and a space heater to warm the house. They would go out in the night, so the frost would be thick on the windows by the morning. My dad would get up and start a fire in both stoves, and then he'd call my cousin (who lived with us after his mother died) and me to get up. We'd grab our clothes, run downstairs and put our clothes in the oven to warm them up before dressing and heading outside. We milked 12 cows by hand daily and hand separated the milk and the cream.

In 1936, after a huge snowstorm and a 20-below-zero temperature, I had to scoop a path from the cow barn to the tank, so the cows could go out for water. They couldn't stay out very long or their teats would freeze. While they were out, we'd hurry and clean out the manure, feed them grain and hay, and rebed the straw so they'd be comfortable.

After big winter snowstorms, two or three neighbors would come across my grandparent's land by bobsled, put their horses in our barn, and they and Dad would hitch a team to go to town. It was about 2 miles to get groceries or some coal, if it was available at the lumberyard.

Starting in 1937, our family saw much technology enter our lives. That was the year Dad got his first John Deere Model B; what a deal, it could pull two 12" plows. To think of that today is not overly impressive, but back then, it was great. The REC (Rural Electric Cooperative) came thru our area around 1938; we had one bulb in each room! Soon after that, we got our first Dehaval milking machine–wow! Then, we finally had water piped into the house about 1946, and we built on a bathroom because of it; it sure was great to not have to go out to the "two-holer" anymore.

We hardly ever missed church; we even went by sled some-times until Dad got his first car. It was, I believe, a new Model A in 1931 for the huge price of $600 at the most.

Life was tough in those days, but we survived and probably were better families because of it.

The Balance Sheet

By Joe Millard

It was 1939, and my family was renting an 80-acre farm; half was tillable, half was a woody, hilly pasture. The farm was located one mile north and three miles west of Jefferson, Iowa. The farm buildings are now gone. The Raccoon River ran south of the farm about one mile, a small meandering creek ran through the pasture that fed into the Raccoon. The wooded pasture was ideal for building log cabins. Sometimes, we built mud dams on the stream to make small ponds; we caught minnows in them to use as bait for fishing in the Raccoon.

We were so isolated. The Pacific Fleet was safely harbored in Pearl Harbor, a crazy man in Germany was causing trouble for Europe, and my parents were placing hope in Franklin Roosevelt to bring better times to the United States and to Green County, Iowa.

The 1930s depression provided an unforgiving hardship for many people in Iowa. Farms were lost and many peoples' futures were changed forever. However, we never went to bed hungry, never thought we were poor and always felt loved. We were scrubbed clean when we attended Mass in our Sunday clothes.

After our father's death, I discovered a "1939 Farm Income and Expense Ledger" kept by our mother. Detailed information revealed much of what living was like for our family in 1939. Copied here is that balance sheet:

1939 Balance Sheet

Source of Income	Amt. Received	Expenditure	Amt. of Expenditure
Sale of Cream	$ 108.34	All Groceries	$ 180.74
Sale of Chickens	$ 44.22	Church Contributions	$ 8.10
Glen's Day Labor	$ 95.88	Clothing	$ 86.02
Sale of Eggs	$ 131.61	Gas	$ 73.17
Farm Income*	$ 739.26	Kerosene	$ 5.61
Balance from 1938	$ 1,211.31	Spiegel Payments	$ 36.54
		Misc. Expense	$ 106.65
Total Income	$ 1,211.31	Farm Expenses**	$ 676.93
		Oil	$ 3.27
* Sale of Livestock & Grain		Dentist/Dr. Bills	$ 13.80
		Misc. Farm Items	$ 18.16
		Total Expenditure	$ 1,208.99
		** Rent and Farm Expenses	
Total 1939 Income	$ 1,211.31		
Total 1939 Expend.	$ 1,208.99		
Bal. to begin 1940	$ 2.32		

January 1, 1940

Winds blow across the plains,
War ravishes Europe, and
Involvement preaches responsibility

Wizard wins an Oscar,
Washington hatches the New Deal, and
Isolationist's advocate safeness

World War II is a year away, and
There is $2.32 to start the year,
Iowa farmers hurt.

Memories of Douglas #1

By Shirley Muench Beam

The rural school was the center of the educational, political and social system of rural Iowa. I am proud to have played a small part in this drama.

During the 1951-1952 school year, I taught at Douglas #1 located south of the S curve off Highway 63. It was destroyed a couple years later due to consolidation and busing. This ended a special era of education practiced since colonial days.

Then, you could teach with as few as five quarters of college. In the 1940s, a high school graduate who passed a competency test could teach. Teacher training programs were a common part of a high school curriculum–they were called "Normal Schools." I attended Iowa State Teacher's College at Cedar Falls for five quarters. Looking back, it seems like a formidable task to be the administration, faculty, playground supervisor and janitorial staff at age 19! All this, and my salary was only $1,875 for the year. However, I had attended Douglas #2 for my first eight years, so this was not foreign to me.

The layout of most rural schools was similar. The entryway included coat hooks, lunch pail (usually syrup pails) shelves and the Red Wing water cooler. We had no running water, so I brought water from my home 4 miles away. Between the doors leading into the classroom hung the rope for ringing the bell. I don't remember ever ringing it, because the kids were always on time, and I was outdoors with them at recess time.

The classroom was sparsely furnished. A nearly bare bookshelf was in the back corner. Individual student desks faced the blackboard at the front. I had only 12 students, so the room was not crowded. Pictures of Washington and Lincoln were hung by the diagonally shaped clock. "Palmer Method" alphabet cards were posted above the blackboard. There was the oil burner, my desk and a small arrangement of chairs for individual classes. Tall, narrow windows lined each side of the room and were necessary before the availability of electricity.

The school grounds were as sparsely equipped as the classroom. The building site was about a half acre with only homemade swings and a teeter-totter for equipment. Two outhouses sat behind and away from the school.

Despite the facilities, learning was taking place. The curriculum emphasized the basics: reading, writing and arithmetic. Students quickly learned that they were expected to work independently. Each grade's daily assignments were written on the blackboard. They were to read the instructions and begin working. If a new unit or concept was assigned, I met with that grade for explanation and discussion. This arrangement worked well for the upper grades, since they could concentrate for longer periods of time. My four kindergarten boys needed a variety of hands-on activities. It took a lot of time to prepare meaningful seat work for them. We used the workbook series "Puzzle Pages," a sophisticated series of lessons in categorizing, sequencing and fine motor activities. We used a hectograph to make multiple copies. A special indelible pencil was used to write the text. The paper was then pressed, face down, on a jelly-like pad that would absorb the ink. The original paper would be removed, and a blank paper would be pressed on to pick up the ink from the jelly. This was repeated to make duplicates. This procedure made for wonderful conversations in later years when my colleagues complained about the blackline copier.

To graduate from eighth grade, students had to pass county-administered competency tests. We spent much time preparing for them. Both of my boys passed on their first try, so they participated in the county-wide graduation ceremony. They were so proud!

Our curriculum was pretty basic, but we had a few enrichment activities. We had physical education every day, art on Fridays and music twice a week–always a total disaster! I especially liked physical education; most my students were boys, so we played a lot of action games such as Pom-Pom Pull Away,

Red Rover, Whip the Rope, Last Man Out and softball. We'd cross the road to play in an open field. I remember one game in particular. I was playing catcher and kneeled down to catch the ball just as my 180-pound eighth grader ran towards home. His knee hit me right in the chest, knocking the wind out of me. I couldn't speak for a few minutes–but I still remember the look on his face. I'm sure he thought he had killed the teacher!

Art wasn't exactly an exercise in creativity, but was a break from the routine. We made seasonal decorations, using construction paper and water colors, and gifts for parents at Christmas. Music was a definite weakness. We had a list of required songs and the accompanying records that usually featured mature female voices. The kids were to sing along to show that they knew the words. The older boys hated the whole thing, and I could understand! I lacked musical talent, so I was no help.

At Christmas, we had a program for the parents. We picked holiday plays, poems and familiar songs. For a few weeks, we turned the school into a theater. The performance was far from polished, but it was a really big deal to speak in front of a crowd. The parents brought treats and seemed to enjoy the "grand performance," no matter how humble! The kids exchanged gifts, and Santa came with a little bag of candy for all.

The parents played an important role in their children's education. They taught them respect for others and for learning. Discipline was certainly no problem; the kids were there to learn and they knew it! At home, students were learning responsibility by being involved in all phases of homemaking and farming operations. They learned life skills from day one.

Over my 30-year teaching career, I went from a one-room school with twelve students to a large urban school with 1,800 students. I've seen many changes in education, but the one year I spent at Douglas #1 has always been very special to me.

An Eighth-Grade Examination

By Joe Millard

The recent interest in standardized testing for students is not new to Iowa. Currently, the University of Iowa is a national leader in elementary and high school testing with the Iowa Test of Educational Development and the Iowa Test of Basic Skills. What may not be known, however, is that in the 19th and 20th centuries, students attending Iowa rural schools were required to take an eighth-grade examination prior to being admitted to a city high school.

The State Eighth-Grade Examination was given to 23 eighth-grade students who attended rural schools in Greene County, Iowa, on May 5, 1950. On that day, these 23 students met at the Greene County Courthouse for a day of testing and were expected to pass the test before being admitted to high school. Nineteen were from one-room schools in Bristol, Grant, Greenbrier, Highland, Jackson and Willow townships, and four were from St. Mary's, a parochial school located in Grand Junction. The

County School Superintendent, R.A. Morris, and his assistant, Florence Huffman, were there to administer the day-long ordeal. There were five tests with 544 questions measuring a student's knowledge and understanding in reading, arithmetic, language, social studies, science and health. The students also had to answer 10 music questions prepared by Greene County educators. The tests were timed, and students were given a noon break to eat their sack lunch before continuing the tests. A review of the questions reveals much about the times and what was expected of those 13- and 14-year old students. Here is a brief analysis of the examination.

The reading test examined a student's ability to read and interpret various forms of writing. There were five paragraphs discussing the changes that were taking place in the family, an advertisement for a bike speedometer, a book review, a newspaper story about the White House and an excerpt from the Judy Canova radio broadcast. Students were also asked to interpret a cartoon.

The arithmetic section checked a student's understanding and ability to perform computation. There were a few measurement and graph questions, along with a separate section on vocabulary and mathematical formulas. The vocabulary section asked the meanings of area, lines, the hypotenuse of a right triangle and changing fractions to percentages. While the use of algebra could be used in solving the many computation problems, only one question actually set up an algebraic equation. In addition to the basic computation problems, the arithmetic test required young scholars to solve problems. Here is one such example:

While cultivating corn with a two-row cultivator, a farmer cultivated 80 rows of corn. He knew the rows were a half mile in length.
Approximately how many miles did he travel while cultivating?

1) 40 miles
2) 28 miles
3) 20 miles

4) 80 miles
5) Answer not given

There were 223 questions on the language test–41 percent of the total eighth- grade exam. There were 30 spelling words, 47 language usage questions, 70 punctuation tasks and 76 capitalization items.

The social studies test was very complete with 154 questions. There were questions asking why the Native Americans were called Indians, what was the main reason that the United States feared communism, what U.S. treaties were signed in 1949, and what were the advantages of having many nationalities, religions and cultures in the United States? Students were asked the purpose of labor unions too. There were questions about agriculture, the United States Constitution, the Iowa Board of Regents, Carpetbaggers, the Monroe Doctrine, World War II, the Civil War and the creation of the League of Nations.

While there was no identified geography test, there were social studies questions centered on a map of the United States. The students were expected to know where various agriculture and mining products came from, and where various cities were located. There were also several questions about the climate of the United States. There were no world geography questions. Students were expected to know the meaning of suffrage, boycotting, tributary (of a river), drought, allies, delta, rebates and legislation.

Students were expected to have knowledge about animals, flies and the diseases they carry, weather, immunizations, tooth decay and hygiene practices to complete the science and health test. Students were also expected to read an electric meter. A subtest assessed a student's knowledge of the scientific theory. The science vocabulary test included the words: nutrition, scientific theory, bacteria, quarantine, environment, manufacture and interdependent.

The music exam asked questions about composers like Brahms, Schubert, and Stephen Foster. Students also needed to know the value of various notes and the letter names of the treble staff.

Records show that all the students passed the exam that day; however, all the students did not go on to high school. On May 19, 1950 Jessie M. Parker, State Superintendent of Public Instruction, addressed the class and presented Eighth grade diplomas to the 23 students. Three of those students were recognized as Honor I Students for having done exceptionally well on the test and for their overall eighth-grade academic achievement.

As you can see, standardized testing has been a part of Iowa education for many years.

Country School – One Day – 1936

By Rosalind E. Engel

"Rosalind, time to get up and get ready for school." Mother's call came from downstairs. "It's mighty cold. Be sure to wear long underwear today."

I opened my eyes, yawned, and stretched in my cocoon of blankets and comforters. It didn't seem like morning. It was dark – darker than usual on a February morning at 6:30. Glancing at the window, I understood why. Jack Frost had been busy during the night painting layer upon layer on the window panes.

Closing my eyes to gather courage, I slipped out from under my warm covers into the cold room. The floor was icy under my bare feet. With a quick step and a shuffle, I gathered my clothes, then ran down the stairs into my mother's bedroom, where I stood like a statue over the register, enjoying the luxury of the hot air billowing out my flannel nightgown and smoothing the goose bumps on my legs. *I knew Mother would have risen early to fire the furnace with chunks of wood and coal.* Shivers came and went. When my legs were blotched with red, I started dressing.

Long underwear first – I disliked wearing it – only feet, hands,

and head sticking out. Long, brown, cotton stockings, next. Such a bother to try to get them smooth at the ankles. One hand held the fold of underwear, while the other tried to draw the stocking over and up. It never failed, there were always bulges and wrinkles. A band of elastic held the stocking above the knee. The remaining top of the stocking had been rolled over the elastic. Bloomers, then, made of gold sateen, which I dutifully pulled over my knees for warmth. I would push them up later, when out of Mother's sight. Shoes, high shoes for winter, were laced and tied. Next, my one wool dress, which was worn every cold day of winter. *My mother was frugal and clever with sewing. This dress, like many of my other clothes, had been made from hand-me-downs from cousins much, much older than I.* To keep my wool dress clean, I covered it with an apron, a plain kind of pinafore, which could be washed and ironed with relative ease. My sister, in high school now, helped with the buttons in the back. She was the one who combed *and pulled* my blonde locks. The night before, she had wrapped my hair around long, metal curlers and snapped the wires shut. I'm sure there were grooves in my head from lying on them all night, but that was the price of Shirley Temple curls. This was 1936, and the popular, little movie star was copied by many. I saw her pictures in magazines and heard about her on the radio, but, during my eight years of life, I had not seen a movie. Movies must be exciting. *My older brothers talked about the movies they had seen at the Opera House in Arlington. One had even won a hundred dollars on a bank night.*

There, I was dressed, and it was close to breakfast time. I could smell the pork chops as they browned in the heavy, iron frying pan. I could hear the rhythm of the spoon against the crockery as the pancake batter was beaten. The kitchen was cozy from the heat of the cook stove.

Since my brothers and Dad were not yet in from milking and cleaning the barn, and separating the cream from the milk in the shed attached to the house, I had time to prepare my lunch for school. In the bottom of the sorghum pail, I placed an apple, homegrown and stored in the cellar. Mother always had cookies on hand that she had baked, and I could choose one large one. I wrapped it in waxed paper. Next, the sandwiches. What kind today–peanut butter or fried egg? There was cheese, of course, but I didn't care for that. I decided on peanut butter. Mother had prepared a new batch. She always took the peanut butter from the container together with the oil that floated on top and mixed it well. Then, she added honey or syrup and mixed that all together. It made a real treat and wasn't so sticky in your throat. Two slices of homemade bread—*I'd like to have boughten sometime.* Mom sliced it, 'cause mine always turned out crooked—thick and thin. I layered it with butter and peanut butter, put the top on, cut it in half, and wrapped it in waxed paper. Then, lid on the pail, and lunch was ready.

I took a moment to look out the window. Unbelievable! The blizzard that had raged the entire weekend had quieted, and the world outside was one like I had never seen. Gone were all the familiar objects. Everything was covered with a lumpy blanket of white. Gone was the hill on which the barn stood. The valley was totally filled in, and my brothers, coming out of the barn, walked right on top. Their tracks were barely noticeable. I looked for the fence around the pigpen. All the posts and wire had disappeared. Where was the lane?

During breakfast, my brothers had many stories to tell about the storm and the snow, as they wolfed down pancakes and chops. Mother kept her station at the cook stove baking eight at a time, and each time a stack was brought to the dining room table, it disappeared in an instant. 'Twas a marvel to me, how they could east so-o much. I was never hungry for breakfast, but I was told it was important to eat that meal. I'd look for a small pancake and put a generous amount of butter and homemade maple syrup or molasses on top. Since I loved meat, if I took a bite of meat with each bite of pancake, I could get it down. Then the big white cup of milk had to be drunk. In my eight years of life I had learned that it did absolutely no good to dawdle, so I'd drink it as fast as I could. *It was whole milk, of course. Had it stood, a thick layer of cream would rise to the top. Mother would use that in baking or would serve it plain or whipped on desserts. The rest of the milk, which was not brought in the house, was separated. The cream was sold, and the skim milk was given to the pigs.*

I overheard my brothers wondering if the hard drifts would hold up the horses. The cows had not sunk in when they were turned out in the yard to get a drink from the tank. *The tank was heated that morning to melt the ice.* They talked of hitching the horses to the bobsled, and I heard them say that if it worked, they would take me to school. The temperature was below zero, and they thought I might freeze my face or feet walking the three-quarters of a mile.

Excitement filled me clear down to my toes! I hoped they would hurry out to the barn to try their plan. They'd have to scoop the bobsled out of the snow first. I hurried to wash my face and brush my teeth so I'd be ready. I gathered my five-buckled overshoes, my heavy wool coat, stocking cap, two pairs of mittens, and a wool scarf. Mother put traveling blankets by the door.

I watched the progress from the kitchen window. After the beginning struggles of the horses to break the runners loose from having been frozen to the ground and trampling in the deep snow that had been disturbed, the horses got their footing on top of the hard drifts, not even sinking in. Those horses were so big and heavy plus the weight of the bobsled – I couldn't believe what I was seeing!

I hurried to put on my outside clothes. I was hardly able to move and must have resembled a big, dark snowball rolling slowly toward the sled. The outside air was sharp and icy. My eyes were the only part of me exposed, but I could tell by the stinging sensation in them that it was very, very cold. Once in the box of the sled, I would close them for seconds at a time for protection from the cold and the glare. But, I didn't want to miss anything, so instead of staying wrapped in my blankets seated on the floor, I would stand often to take in the glistening beauty of the pure, breath-taking landscape and to see what feats Bert and Bess, the huge draft horses, could accomplish.

We rode over fences and hazelnut brush. We knew it had to be down under there somewhere. There were no ditches or roads to be seen. The tops of tall evergreen groves protected the neighboring farm scenes and were our only landmarks. Then my school came into view. I had never reached school so fast and with such fun. Little did I know that the winter of '36 would go down in Iowa history as the *bad* one. It seemed like such a good one at that moment.

Smoke curled from the chimney of the Meisgeier School. Somehow the teacher had made her way across the fields and had managed to clear a narrow path from the woodshed to the schoolhouse door, so she could bring in fuel to start the fire. The stove stood in the middle of the room toward the back. Perhaps some men from nearby farms had helped. That didn't matter to me! When we arrived, and the door was opened, the glow of the stove's belly, the sunlight filtering through the frosty windows, and the teacher's smile fairly propelled me in! We were safe from the bitter cold in our little one-room shelter in the midst of that vast world of white.

Two of the boys were sent to the closest farm, a quarter mile away, for water for drinking and washing hands, as was the usual practice. Lunches were not placed in the cloakroom as was usual. That was too far from the stove. The lunches needed to thaw.

A rearrangement of the room took place. The teacher moved her station from the front on the stage to a double desk near the stove. All of the nine students, who usually occupied single desks near the front, were allowed to move back into the double desks. We had always longed for that opportunity, but now realized, two people in the same desk could be tricky. Both had to be ready to raise the top of the desk or close it at the exact same time. The temptation to whisper would be great, but the warmth of the stove was necessary.

Precisely at nine o'clock, the teacher pulled the rope attached to the big, black, iron bell in the belfry, proclaiming to the neighborhood that school was now in session. We stood by our desks to say the pledge to the flag, which was positioned in the front, right corner of the room. Then, absolute quiet prevailed as recitations began. The lower grades went first. Assignments had been written on the blackboard to keep the others busy.

Not all eight grades were represented with our nine students. I was the smartest and the slowest student in the fifth grade – the only one. Previous teachers had tried to do something about that. One decided to hurry me through second grade in a half of the school year, so I could be with two others in third. I finished third grade with them at the end of the year. We were together again in fourth grade for a few months. Then one dropped out because of a serious illness, never to return, and the other moved away in March, which was the typical time for farm families to move to other farms. I was alone in my grade again *and for the rest of my country school days.*

I looked up from writing to collect my thoughts. I noticed one of the older girls was waving one finger in the air. The teacher nodded affirmatively. The girl bundled up, boots and all, for the trek *on* the snow to the girl's outhouse in the far corner of the schoolyard. The boy's outhouse was located in the opposite corner. Evidently, someone had shoveled the snow around the door so it would open. This was the one time the teacher didn't have to look at her watch and record the student's name on the board for punishment later if she took too long. Severe cold makes for great haste when toileting under those conditions. Of course, the teacher allowed more time when two fingers were raised. I was glad I didn't have to go yet.

In between classes, the teacher added more coal to the fire. Even so, the cold that seeped in around the windows and through the cracks began to penetrate our bodies. I rubbed my fingers together to warm them and wanted to tap my toes. Occasionally, a shiver shook my spine.

Recess time came and went. It was too cold to play outdoors, the teacher announced. We didn't think so. Pump-pump-pull-away would have been great fun on top of the snow. Instead, we paused only for stretching, getting drinks, and for those who needed to make quick trips to the far corners. Then all was quiet again.

At lunchtime, we stayed close by the stove and told stories about how high the snow was drifted at our houses as we ate. Fish stories couldn't compete with these elaborations. Lunch tasted so good. Soon we heard the snowplow roaring by. We ran to the windows, peeking through the frost to watch the banks grow high on each side of the plow's path. This was the main gravel to town three miles away, so it was opened before the side roads. Often the plow had to back up and crash the drift again before it was able to cut through. We felt like cheering when it was successful.

It was then, the teacher decided she would dismiss us early that day. She was chilled, too. She wrote a note and sent two volunteers to the farmhouse close by, asking that they call the telephone operator and have a general ring announcing our dismissal. All our families and more, twenty-three altogether, were on the telephone line. For each, we cranked a different combination of shorts and longs. Mine was three longs. Many would dash to the phone, hanging on the wall in the kitchen or dining room, whenever it rang to listen in, but if there was a general ring, which was very long, everyone listened. General rings brought important announcements, and the one today would give our dismissal time.

Our parents would have been home that day anyway to receive us, and mothers were almost always home, but time was very important in such severe weather. One could freeze appendages walking those distances.

None of us were unhappy thinking about being dismissed early. We had visions of playing on/in the snow, sliding, making angels, building forts, whatever. We dismissed the cold. *Of such is the logic of children!*

We settled once more to the strict quiet imposed upon us while studying. One of the quiet rules was: If you dropped something, you must stand in the front of the schoolroom holding that object for twenty minutes, thinking about your disturbance of the quiet.

Something dropped! It was a tiny sound. It was near my desk. I didn't drop anything! The teacher's keen ears didn't miss it. She spotted the object at the same moment as I. A sprung bobby pin lay on the floor beside my desk. I reached up to feel my hair. The bobby pin that held the curls back from my face was gone! It had slipped out of my hair.

In a moment, I found myself standing on the stage with that pin in my hand. My head was bowed, my face was red, and I'm sure that more than one tear fell from my eyes. Luckily, the teacher couldn't hear those! I can't describe all the feelings I was fighting inside. Anger and embarrassment were two. How could I ever face my parents and tell them I had been punished at school? I didn't mean to make any noise. I was angry with my sister for selecting the wrong pin to draw back my hair. I was angry with the teacher for punishing me for something I couldn't control. I was afraid I would be teased forever by the other kids. The twenty-minute time period was an eternity, and even though, I was standing in the cold front of the room, I was too distraught to shiver. Finally, I was dismissed to my desk. The rest of the day faded away!

Early dismissal came. We all bundled ourselves in our heavy outer clothes. The teacher helped with the scarves around our faces. Nine stuffed mannequins trudged out of the door, walking on the snow over the deep ditch to the road, then following the snowplow's path with its high walls on either side. Life became adventurous again in this unfamiliar world.

In a quarter of a mile, when I reached my turn-off, I beheld a wonderful surprise! There stood Bert and Bess, their heads partially enveloped in breath-clouds and their hoofs stepping nervously in place. My big brothers helped me into the bobsled, and off we went again, sliding over the fences and the hazelnut brush in a direct route to where the tall, pine grove sheltered our farm scene. Never mind roads and lanes! And since our road was not considered a main thoroughfare, it would remain blocked and would provide adventures for days to come. With snow excitement renewed, the trauma of my afternoon at school diminished – for the moment!

Rural History

The Transmission of Rural Values

By Paul Lasley

Most college students take rural sociology courses to meet a university requirement for a certain number of social science credits. In over 20 years of teaching, I have struggled many times to make rural sociology "come alive" to reluctant students. I have found that my profound lectures about rural values and beliefs generally fall upon deaf ears. It was in the struggle to make my course more interesting that I developed a class exercise to help many students understand the importance of rural values and how they are passed down across generations. My grandmother Sadie was fond of adages and sayings. She had one for every situation, it seemed. It was not until adulthood that I began to reflect on the values that she was trying to instill in my siblings and me.

So for the next few minutes try this exercise, I would tell my students. Relax and listen–listen for the voices of your parents (or grandparents) with what they told you about how to live or work. Recall the advice they gave you about being success-ful, how to treat others or why to save money. Listen for their maxims about life. Your assignment is to write down a favorite adage and explain its meaning.

Over the years, this assignment has provided much richness in my rural sociology classes. With some encouragement, stu-dents begin to share their family's words of wisdom and advice. Here are some of my favorites. Some are common, others are original, and some are just fun.

- Even a blind pig will find an acorn once in a while.
- An idle mind is the devil's workshop.
- Early to bed, early to rise makes a person healthy, wealthy and wise.

- A stitch in time saves nine.
- The early bird gets the worm.
- A penny saved is a penny earned.
- Don't kick a gift horse in the mouth.
- Don't judge a book by its cover.
- You can lead a horse to water, but you can't make it drink.
- Experience is the best teacher, it ought to be, it is the most expensive.
- The fruit never falls far from the tree.
- Where there is a will, there is a way.
- Birds of feather flock together.
- Make hay when the sun shines.
- Haste makes waste.
- An angry man opens his mouth and shuts his eyes.
- Idleness is the root of all evil.
- Choose your love and love your choice.
- In some situations it is better to remain silent and let others think you are a fool than to speak out and erase all doubt.
- A man of words and not deeds is like a garden full of weeds.
- As you make your bed, so must you lie in it.
- A fool and his money are soon parted.
- There is nothing common about common sense.
- Hope for the best, get ready for the worst and then take what God chooses to send.
- Fools rush in where angels fear to tread.
- In the land of the blind, the one-eyed man is king.
- You can't make an omelet without breaking some eggs.
- Let sleeping dogs lie.
- What is learned in the cradle lasts 'til the grave.
- Get up with the rooster and go to bed with the cows.
- He squealed like a pig caught under a gate.
- It's a hard row to hoe.
- You can't make a silk purse out of a sow's ear.
- We're eating high on the hog.

- We are in high cotton.
- They have more faults than a pine board has knots.
- He's blinking his eyes like a bullfrog in a hail storm.
- It's harder for some to deal with success than adversity.
- He's too big for his britches.
- Blessed are those that run in circles for they shall be called wheels.
- He's a chip off the old block.
- Even a stopped clock is right twice a day.
- Things that go around come around.

This exercise has proven effective in three ways. First, it highlights rural values that parents or grandparents have instilled in their children. Second, it brings into focus how values are transmitted across generations. And third, it provides many examples of important values that persist in contemporary rural society. The process of how wisdom is transmitted across generations brings a sociological perspective on familial communication that takes on new meaning when it can be grounded in personal experiences. The values of hard work, honesty, integrity and faith are common elements in the adages my students shared. Historically, rural culture was an oral one, where stories, metaphors and adages played a large role in the upbringing of children. The values we learned through maxims or adages in our childhood are likely the ones that we will pass on to our children and grandchildren.

Editor's Note: Paul Lasley is Professor and Chair of the Sociology Department at Iowa State University, Ames

The Death of a Country Church

By Adeline Sanden Jones

The autumn air was as still as death, but golden rays of sunshine were pouring through the windows; rich farm fields ready to be harvested wrapped their arms around us like a comforting quilt. We had all gathered for the funeral of Bristol Lutheran Church. Many questions ran through our heads. Why? Why do we have to give up our beautiful country church with its many memories of our childhood? It's sacred! "What God has joined together, let no man put asunder," I thought.

I didn't hear much of what Rev. Stoa and Rev. Peters said that day–instead, I was recalling the happy and the sad occasions I had been a part of in this huge, simple, beautiful country church. As a child, I remembered running up and down the steps before and after Sunday School, sitting with Grandmother during services (we had to sit on the left side of the church as an old Norwegian custom dictated that the men and women never sat together to worship), Mom always playing the organ, being active as a teenager in Luther League, making eyes at a favorite boyfriend, as an organist playing for a funeral in Norwegian when I can't read Norwegian, coming back to attend services with the whole family, baptisms, weddings, funerals–all memories never to be forgotten!

The church was full of people today; extra chairs were set up, just like it had been for the past 92 years!

Why, O God, does this church have to be torn down? The roof was leaking, the furnace needed repair, the expenses of heating were great, and the salary of the minister and organist had to be met. My mind is jogged back to reality. Was I being practical or selfish? I simply didn't wish for a big part of my life to be suddenly jerked from under me. There were about 25 church members–couldn't they afford to keep my memories alive? As my whole life passed before me, I realized that nothing on this earth is immortal–you plant a seed, it grows (if nourished), the harvest is great but when the harvest is finished, it dies. But wait, it has produced seeds of its own, and the cycle is repeated.

As the few members of Bristol carried the furnishings and vessels from the altar, down the aisle, tears streaming down their faces and the faces of the people who were there for the funeral, our hearts were heavy with sadness.

No, Bristol Lutheran Church has not died, it has produced thousands of seeds and one of the seeds will be planted at Our Savior Lutheran Church in Federal Dam, Minnesota. The altar, the altar rail, the paraments, the pulpit, the organ and the pews will come alive in their new church, bringing joy and memories to thousands of others. Bristol Lutheran Church will live on forever!

The cemetery where loved ones lie in peace, side by side, enclosed by the peaceful fields will always be there, a reminder to us that our roots remain.

A Stroll Across Hillside Farm

By Kent Baker

Notes while hiking across Hillside Farm, south of Moville ...

This is where I was raised–spent the first 17 years of my life before I hurried away to what I saw as greener pastures... . Greener pastures? How foolish... . There could be no greener pastures than those of this dark, fertile, Iowa land. There are easier pastures, more productive pastures, more amiable pastures, but certainly, none that could be greener.

The name of the farm always seemed just so right. Perched on the hillside above the lush valley of the West Fork of the Little Sioux River, the land rose sharply from the road that separated the flat valley from its eastern hills.

Rolling prairie, the homesteaders called it. Part of the greatest unbroken, unspoiled expanse of land found anywhere in the world–that area of this wonderful new, pure continent that was to become the breadbasket to the world. A land distinguished by the wonderfully rich soil that would feed billions. A land nurtured by its native peoples. Absolutely unspoiled.

Hiking into the fields, away from signs of civilization, away from the bustle of the highway, away from the farmstead where good men still till the earth, away from the electric lines, one can still see the land as the pioneers saw it. Marvelous. Quiet. Stretching endlessly. Verdant. Grasses swaying in the ever-present wind.

Having come from the worn-out lands of Europe, how wonderful this rolling prairie must have seemed to those people of no fear.

I pick a piece of grass and stick it in my mouth. It tastes sweet, as I remember. And then I smell the hay. Is there any more distinctive or sweeter smell in nature than that of newly-cut hay?

My friends in other places would laugh and not understand. What is hay?

Baling hay was one of those hot, dirty, physical, wearying jobs of childhood that has been almost entirely eliminated by mechanization.

I stroll through a grove on the original homestead, far away from today's modern farm home and buildings. Here the trees are 100 years old. Trees, of course, that weren't part of that amazing prairie that greeted our forefathers. For the prairie rolled on without any broken soil to allow trees or bushes. Only the prairie grasses and wildflowers. But those forefathers needed shade from the scorching summers and windbreaks from the freezing winters, so they planted acres and acres of trees in formal rows. Many of those old groves haven't survived as the economics of today's farms have forced its guardians to produce from every possible acre to meet the financial demands of the stewardship of the land. But here, at least, stand the stately survivors. And on this hot and sultry day, the grove casts a wonderful cooling shade over this native son.

And the birds. The air is silent but for the whispers of the wind ... and the presence of the birds. Even at this age, here, I'm a child again, trying to learn the different sounds, trying to recognize from a glance what bird is what.

Of course, through the hike there are reminders of other times past. The name of the farm, as many know, wasn't always Hillside Farm. It was Hillside Turkey Farm, part of the biggest industry in this area through 40 years. In the days when Iowa led the nation in the production of turkeys, Moville was one of the major centers. Millions of turkeys a year produced on dozens of farms scattered around the area. That, too, is gone today; a remnant of history, a victim – as with so many things – of economic forces over which the farmer had no control.

Left as witnesses of this proud history are abandoned (or converted) turkey sheds and brooder houses that dot the hilltops in the Moville region.

These are just changes in time. Changes in life. But when one thinks of the hard work that went into building that industry ...

when one thinks of the families that participated in that industry … of the billions of pounds of meat that were produced right here and sent around the world for consumption, one can't help but be a bit nostalgic.

I turn back toward that verdant valley, toward the civilization of today's rural America, toward the "new" homestead, with its young stewards engaged in the work of the land.

There's little value in a hike back in time. Oh, it can be a bit relaxing. It can bring back wonderful memories. But today should be lived for today. Our thoughts should be with the people of today, the issues of today, the complexities of today.

But, for a few moments in those green fields, there was a chance to remember and reflect. And I did.

Editors Note: Kent Baker is President/Owner of the Moville Record, Moville, Iowa, where this column first appeared. He left his western Iowa home many years ago to work at newspapers and television stations elsewhere. In 2000, he returned to his home state and region.

Barn to Ashes

By Monte Sesker

More than a barn turned to smoke that spring night in 1990. A thunderstorm swept away family farm "treasures" and left nothing but memories glowing in the early morning ashes, which were all that remained of the barn that Grandpa Charlie Hanks had built more than 100 years earlier. Grandpa Charlie's barn literally exploded from the direct lightning hit, recounted a neighbor, who called the town of Cambridge Volunteer Fire Department.

Trucks arrived just minutes after the phone rang in our bedroom located on the opposite side of the house. I scrambled to the kitchen window and saw the hay mow door outlined by orange flames; there was no chance to save it.

A few hours later, I was perched next to the pump house under the old windmill staring at nothing but the limestone foundation. Crisp dawn air mixed with the acrid smell of the smoldering black mass filled my lungs and thoughts of what the barn represented filled my mind. I had spent much of my youth here; hours upon hours were passed in and around the barn, which was once the center of the farm operation's economy.

My wife Carolyn and I had purchased the farm from the estate in 1965, so our children also harbor their own "barnhood" memories. In a sense, it was like losing an old friend. If you lived, worked or played on an Iowa farm as a child or young adult, you can relate to some of these random thoughts.

By barn standards, the structure was medium-sized, the board and bat exterior was held together by 12" x 12" pegged oak beams. Kept in good shape, it was a local "landmark," one of the few still standing in the area. And yep, it was me that nearly upset the wooden-framed hoist once when I forgot how far the axle of the old "B" John Deere protruded outside the inset wheels. Sorry, Grandpa!

Built on a slight rise, part of its upper level once sheltered horses. Molly and Babe, the big draft team, beckoned for handouts through the top half of the Dutch doors. I remember how they earned their oats hitched to a turnstile that operated a chain hoist which lifted wagons to dump grain into the elevator; no soybeans back then. I can still see those big horses stepping over the spinning rod, never missing a beat, walking around and around.

After the corn harvest, the team would move to the field, pulling the straight wagon, reigns tied next to the driverless seat. They'd walk methodically down the corn rows stopping and starting at Grandpa's command. We'd walk alongside tromping stalks, searching for the corn the single-row Woods Bros. picker had missed. The wagon's high bang board rattled with the sound of every ear tossed against it.

The stalls the workhorses shared were eventually filled with my pony that then became my riding horse. Funny how history repeats itself; years later the ponies belonged to my kids and their Grandpa, my father.

A few steps up from the barn's horse stalls and mangers was the large, open hay floor. Near the back, some loose hay still remained which was just fuel for the fire. Stacked high at times, the soft pile was a perfect place for kids to slide. Hay and straw bales covered the rest of the floor. Horses tugged the heavy rope lifting and dropping bales from the fork traveling along the rails attached to the gable; it took a lot of sweat to pick and stack them.

The barn was where forts were built and games of "hide and seek" were played. The towering tiers of beams were also great places to run along in a game of tag. If you slipped, it was okay, because there was usually hay below. The beams and dangling hay rope provided the thrill of swinging like "Tarzan" and dropping into the hay.

As livestock numbers dwindled, the barn's hay floor became a basketball court. A homemade hoop nailed to the wall provided some hot games during cold winter months.

The loft above the horse stalls held sacks of feed, supplement, rolls of twine and chicken wire. Catching and "taming" pigeons was another activity of the time. Most were eventually freed, but they didn't know it–they'd return to perch on your shoulder and beg for feed. Back then, well-armed "BB" gun toters were welcomed to dispatch unwelcome, messy sparrows and starlings; bats that sometimes hung in the darkest corners, however, were too "scary" to bother.

My sons helped their grandfather feed the ponies. New pocket knives in hand, they cut the twine on as many bales as they could find. After all, they had watched him do it–a couple of bales at a time; fresh instructions soon came.

Below the hay floor were milking stanchions, feed bunks, calf stalls and winter shelter for all kinds of farm animals. This is where I first saw a calf born and where my kids learned about foals.

To young minds, the trap door between the upper and lower levels provided more fun than dropping bales to feed the cows below; Tarzan, again. The movie which cost a dime in the Cambridge Theater provided plenty of inspiration. Tarzan trapped animals by placing twigs over a pit, camouflaging them with leaves and then luring unsuspecting animals across. It worked with playmates as well.

In more serious times, Grandpa could milk 8 to 12 Guernseys and Jerseys in rotation just as fast as he could pull. Pails were poured into milk cans and carried up the stone steps to the milk house. A stock tank filled with fresh cold water kept the immersed cans cool for the daily truck that came to pick them up. As much as I tried, I had a hard time mastering milking, let alone the one-legged stool you sat on.

Grandpa chewed Red Man and Beechnut tobacco. Because of this, you had to watch where you stepped even before you shoveled behind the cows.

Bag balm, mentholatum and cans of "this and that" filled the ledge under one window. Cats constantly begged for saucers of warm milk, and sometimes an especially annoying feline would get a squirt in the eye direct from the source. It was a way in which Grandpa liked to show off.

Other than ponies and horses, the old barn also became our storage shed. The fire claimed countless "artifacts" being stored. There were harnesses of all types, bridles, saddles, bicycles, Little Red coaster wagons, antique tools, stock tanks, feeders, electric fences, sleds, the bullet-riddled, horse-shaped weathervane, lots of reclaimed lumber, metal, etc. If you needed something and were willing to search, you could usually find it in there.

There's a large landscaped yard full of trees on the site where the barn and feedlot once stood. Like so many farms, other physical things have changed. The silo is gone; the milk house became a playhouse; the crib was converted to a farm shop (now a retreat for this old woodworker); and the hog houses and wooden machine shed were torn down. The chicken house is now a "garden shed."

The house Grandpa remodeled in 1906 was recycled by us in 1976. Except for the barn, Grandpa would have approved. When he was in his 80s, one of those traveling salesman came calling. The normally conservative, astute man was talked into making a purchase for his barn. I wonder what happened to the guy who sold and installed those lightning rods. I also wonder if one of our grandchildren might live here someday and what changes he or she might make.

A short distance from downtown Cambridge, this old barn was also a playground for local youngsters through the decades. Mom and OSHA sure wouldn't have approved of a lot that happened in there, and I certainly don't want to know what our kids did in there.

Going out the door the morning it burned, I instinctively grabbed a camera; a throwback to my journalism training at ISU and as Editor of Wallace's Farmer. I took a cover photo and wrote a story for the magazine...I'd rather have kept the barn.

Auctions

By LaVern Patterson

"What are you going to bid for it? What are you going to give me? Twenty, twenty, twenty–who'll give twenty to start the bidding?"

The sonorous tones of the auctioneer draw people like flies to honey. You look around and can read people's minds: "Is there something I want to buy?" "Is there a bargain out there for me?" "Look at all this stuff Luella had in her house, where did it all come from?" "I wonder how much Joe will bid for this?" "Why are they bidding so high on that box? There must be something in the bottom of it that I didn't see."

Some of my earliest memories as a child include attending farm auctions with my father and household auctions with my mother. Sometimes there was a particular item that they wanted to purchase, but often they attended because it was a social event attended by neighbors, friends and relatives.

When I was young, there were fewer items on the farm auctions than are found today. Perhaps there would be one or two teams of horses, a harness, a wheeled wagon, a plow, a cultivator, a disc, a harrow and maybe a corn planter. At one household auction when I was 5, the auctioneer took my bid and for a dime I bought a metal-wheeled tricycle and for 50 cents I purchased an old Red Rocket wagon with a wooden tongue. These toys are proudly displayed in our home today.

There are a number of people in an auction staff, including one or more auctioneers who usually have attended a special school. There are two or three clerks to keep track of what is sold and for how much. They also collect the money, pay the bills and balance the finances. Then there are those who hold up the items that are to be sold–the "Vanna Whites" of auctions.

In the mid-1960s, I started writing down what was sold for auctions as part of my duties as an officer at the local bank. This was before the popularity of "collectibles" and "antiques," and people sold fewer items, disposing of most of the small things before the auction. Those who attended the auction were almost entirely made up of people from the local area. I used a yellow tablet and wrote the person's name, the name of the item and the amount bid. At the end of the auction, when a person came to pay for items, we scanned the sheets for their name and added up the amount owed.

As antiques and collectibles became more the vogue and this method of disbursing possessions became more popular, the number of items at each auction increased dramatically, and collectors came from quite a distance. This necessitated a more sophisticated system of clerking. We started using bidding numbers instead of names and special NCR clerking sheets with a heavy copy that could be separated by item and kept in a box under the number of the bidder.

One thing that never changes, however, is the unpredictability of the weather. Country auctions are usually held outdoors. Some days are so hot, we have to wear wet, cool cloths around our necks and seek shade. Other days are so cold that pens won't work, and we have to use pencils to write. Fingers don't work well on those days, and hand warmers are a necessity. Auctions continue to be social events; sometimes visiting between the attendees becomes so loud that a gentle (or not so gentle) reminder has to be given by the auctioneer to quiet down, so they can hear the bids.

It's interesting to watch the bidders; some loudly call out their bids, some wink or wiggle a finger, and there is everything in between. Some people talk with their hands, and bid when they don't mean to. Occasionally you can tell that someone is bidding just because they don't want the other person to have the article, and sometimes a bidder gets carried away by the excitement of bidding and pays much more than intended. There are those who purchase an item for very little money and have such an intense look of excitement that you know they have purchased something of perceived value to them.

At one auction, there was a person from out of state who wanted a certain item and told two different people to buy the item for her, whatever the cost. Both of these people were at the auction and did not know each other. That item brought many times more than it should have.

Auctions are a great place to get delicious homemade pies, too, especially if a church or local group is "lunching" the auction. Who could desire more on a pleasant summer afternoon than homemade pie and coffee, the companionship of friends and neighbors and the excitement of an auction?

City Kid

By Joel Knutson

If you could call my hometown of Red Oak (with a population of 6,000) a city, I was a city kid. In Red Oak, we had close-knit neighborhoods, hard-surfaced roads for biking, sidewalks for roller skating, movie theatres and, as we proudly claimed, the second largest swimming pool in the state of Iowa. Although my country cousins lacked these urban amenities, they made do with diversions of their own: motorbikes, free movies projected onto the side of the local school building and a gravel pit that also may have been the second largest in the state of Iowa. This gravel pit had a makeshift diving board and a notable absence of lifeguards; it was rumored to be hundreds of feet deep in places.

My annual visit to my country cousins on their farm just south of Swaledale was the highlight of my mid to late 1950s summers. I wasn't the only one to come to their farm; our cousins from Minnesota (a region we referred to simply as "up north") also came and visited. Since they were from Rochester, they also bore the unmistakable stamp of "city kids."

For us town folk, the farm was an exotic vacationland. We relished the creek fishing, the homemade go-carts, the fairs and the music festivals. Our host family, Aunt Bert, Uncle Jinx and our cousins Larry, Janet, Bob and Marilyn, indulged us as much as they could. Mostly though, they worked.

It quickly became apparent to young visitors from "the city" that everything and everyone on the farm had to have a purpose, perform a useful function, fill a role of some kind. There was no place for deadwood and no time for deadheads. Our country cousins grew up a lot faster than us, their city counterparts. Back home, I delivered 40 newspapers a day, made my collection rounds on Saturday and then clocked out. On the farm, the clock was of the solar variety. The family worked, more or less, from dawn to dusk and sometimes beyond. An average day for them consisted of early morning chores, a big breakfast, a myriad of household tasks, field work, vet visits, vaccinations, feed grinding, garden tending, putting up hay, de-horning, building and machinery maintenance, evening chores, a hearty dinner, clean-up and, at long last, maybe an hour watching KGLO before my uncle fell asleep in his chair and people began filtering upstairs for a good night's rest, before getting up, and doing it all over again.

On stormy nights, Aunt Bert would fly through the house like a wraith, shutting windows against the rain, wind and hail. I remember staring out the window, thrilled at the meteorological fireworks. Uncle Jinx would stare out the window, too, but he was wondering what he would find in his fields tomorrow.

Jinx was an Oliver man, in the same way that other people were Presbyterians or Baptists. His rolling stock included three tractors, but his pride and joy was a brawny Row Crop 88. He was an Oldsmobile fan, too, favoring a white-over-green Rocket 88 – as pretty and powerful a car as I've seen to this very day.

Jinx was also suspicious of any male over the age of, say, 9 who couldn't drive a tractor; such an individual's usefulness was seriously in doubt. Since I fell squarely into this category, alternatives were arranged for me. I was equipped with a broad-brimmed hat and a corn knife and then deposited at the end of a bean row that I swear was 10 miles long. I spent days flailing away at nasty volunteers until I was mercifully allowed to quit for the day. Back at the house, I'd join the girls for the afternoon, snapping beans and popping peas on the porch.

Worse than working on the farm was the possibility of being exiled to Bible School. Our cousins were of the same denomination as my family, but their little church nearby in Thornton ran the roughest, toughest Bible School God ever invented. In Red Oak, it was plastic lanyards and Kool-Aid. Here, it was chapter and verse and plenty of it. I think we maybe got a 15-minute recess, but I can't swear to it.

In any case, those visits to the farm were voyages of discovery for me. I learned about rock 'n roll from my ultra-cool older cousin, Bob. My younger cousin, Marilyn, joined me once in conducting a solemn funeral for a deceased pig; I read Scripture and heard Marilyn sing.

Everyday occurrences on the farm were strange and shocking to a city kid like me. While exploring the barn, I would plunge through hair-raising dead falls in the hay mow. Out in the feedlots, I would mingle with Hampshires and Herefords. I inspected welding equipment and windmills. One Sunday after church, I looked on in awe as my Uncle Jinx dispatched three rats—three!—with a single blast from his 12 gauge. One memorable morning, I even saw my first fatally bloated steer…right before breakfast. Another day of adventure on the farm had begun!

Special Relationships

Cupid at the Liar's Table

By Paul Lasley

Humor is an important aspect of rural culture. Long before Garrison Keillor brought rural humor to the national spotlight in the NPR Prairie Home Companion, rural life had been the focus of many famous storytellers and writers. Folks such as Minnie Pearl, Will Rogers and Mark Twain, and television shows such as Hee Haw, Beverly Hillbillies and Green Acres popularized rural humor. Generally, it is a humor based on real life experiences mixed with a healthy dose of exaggeration. Often it is hard to distinguish fact from fiction.

In Lancaster, Missouri, my hometown, the local café served as the gathering place for local farmers and merchants to meet every morning. The small town café served the same purpose as in many communities in Iowa and across America. In addition to the usual mix–strong black coffee, cinnamon rolls and ciga-rette smoke–was the banter of exaggeration, pranks, jokes and story telling. The center table in the small café was affectionately known as the Liar's Table. Food and drink were generally second-ary to the social discourse conducted at the Liar's Table. It served as the community news center, a place where friends gathered to discuss recent events, shared local news and from time-to-time played pranks. If you wanted to know what was happening in the community, the Liar's Table was the place to go.

As a summer employee of the local sale barn, I ate lunch every-day at the Liar's Table. I was a young, single college student who had returned home for the summer. While I described my occupa-tion as a sanitation engineer, my real task was hauling manure. A young female nursing student who also had returned home for the summer worked in the café. It didn't seem to make any difference how busy the restaurant was, I always had prompt service from this particular waitress. On each stop, I ordered the daily special and topped off my meal with a piece of homemade pie. I took a good deal of razzing from the older men at the Liar's Table for of the preferential service I received. I claimed it was because of my good looks. They argued I was always served first so that I wouldn't stink up the place. Apparently, the locals readily recognized my presence and occupation by the odors that accompanied me.

That spring, as a fund raiser, the local Methodist Church canvassed the entire town and produced and sold a birthday calendar that included the birthdays of everyone in the community. While I was vaguely aware of the existence of the calendar, I was far too sophisticated to announce my own birthday on July 31. On that day, I was served my daily special and, as usual, ordered a piece of pie. The waitress came back from the kitchen with a rather apologetic demeanor and explained that all the pie was gone! Naturally, I expressed my consternation.

The men at the Liar's Table joined in, proclaiming the cook should be fired, we ought to go to another restaurant where they appreciated their customers and no tips would be left today. The waitress said she would check the kitchen again, but she was pretty certain that there was no pie today. In a couple of minutes, she returned carrying a big birthday cake adorned with candles, as the Liar's Table broke out in singing Happy Birthday. To my complete surprise the Liar's Table, the cook and this cute little waitress had colluded in the birthday surprise. Cake was served to everyone in the café, and I took a good deal of ribbing about my special waitress friend, and how they were able to pull off such a good prank.

This was the beginning of a romance between the waitress and me that lasted throughout the summer. When fall came, I returned to college in Columbia, Missouri, and my special waitress returned to nursing school in Des Moines, Iowa. Two years later, when she and I married in our hometown Baptist church, members of the Liar's Table were among the attending crowd. It may have been the only time that the Liar's Table played cupid. While many of the men of the Liar's Table have passed on in the ensuing 29 years, their prank lives on in our marriage.

Memories of a Farm Wife

By Carolyn Riles

I went from being a country child to a city girl, then back to the country life again when my husband and I married. What a culture shock; but it's been a good trip.

Re-introduction to my country life began with our shivery. For those of you who, like myself, had never heard of a shivery, it is a gathering of country neighbors and friends who arrange the farmer's version of a limo ride around town (i.e. tractor pulls a clean but still fragrant manure spreader with two metal lawn chairs for the newlyweds to sit on, followed by a procession of cars honking to get everyone's attention). An added event was the "iron man wheelbarrow stroll" down Main Street, testing Hubby's ability to drive a load–me–straight. His encouraging words to me were, "Just go along with it honey." Getting into that manure spreader was a bit of a challenge with a straight skirt, but I managed.

Then it was back to our house for lunch, graciously furnished by the ladies, and a chance for the devious ones to do their antics. We were very fortunate to have such a considerate group of people. Rice was in major abundance in the drawers, the sheets, shoes and pockets, and the bed was short-sheeted.

In later years on the farm, when daughters Pam and Kathy were of school age, we had our own special "rock parties." Someone would drive the tractor with a hayrack behind it, and we would all pick up rocks and fill the rack. That was our "aerobic" exercise without having to go to a gym. For variety, we would walk the soybean fields to cut out weeds and stray volunteer corn. That went on for years until Hubby changed to ridge-till, and a total family rebellion brought that phase of farming to an end. It's a tie as to which job the girls disliked most. They still talk about those days to their families.

One wet spring when I was expecting, Murphy's Law prevailed. Hubby's tractor became stuck in the mud. He came up to the house and asked me to go out with him and help pull out the tractor, since rain was forecast for the next day. It took longer for me to get up into the cab than it did to pull him out of the mud.

One fall, when I was helping out in the field, the combine broke shortly before the parts store was to close. It was muddy, and I was supposed to climb on the draw-bar and ride up to the house with Hubby. I somehow slipped off and landed on my back a short distance from the tractor tire. The ground was soft from the recent rain, and the mud oozed up around the tread of the tire as the tractor started to roll back. I yelled at Hubby, but he didn't hear above the noise of the tractor (no cab). I thought it would be my last moment. Fortunately, Hubby saw what had happened and stopped in time. The only thing I could think of was a headline in the newspaper, "Husband runs over wife with tractor."

One summer, we had a small wading pool for the girls in the front yard and had filled it before going to town. When we returned, several sows had escaped their hog lot and found their way to the front lawn. After feasting on my flowering petunias, one of the sows decided that pool was just too big a temptation. She was resting so peacefully with her head on the inflated pool side and stretched out full length in the pool. From a distance it looked as if the sow was smiling–until she saw the car. Suddenly, her four legs moved like a chain saw trying to get traction. That action shredded the pool, and the girls were very unhappy with that pig.

I believe all of our hogs knew when Hubby was going to be gone for the day. That was when they found their escape route. The girls and I would try to get them back in, not always successfully, but at least we kept them off of the road. Hubby raised hogs until the early 1990s when confinements hog houses started multiplying. We both decided we didn't want to go that route and sold out the business.

Farming has changed so much since we first started and will continue to do so long after we retire. It's challenging, rewarding and sometimes heartbreaking; and it is always evolving into something new and different. Farming strengthens and reaffirms your faith in God. Without Him, few things are possible; with Him, the future is limited only to your imagination, ambition and determination.

The Railing

By Marilyn Benson, Summer 1983

The old man began the ascent up the stairs. He wasn't so very old in years but tonight he felt the weight of all his lifetime. As he ascended, his hand automatically reached for the railing.

The railing was the one unique feature of the big, rambling farmhouse. It had been fashioned from a willow out of the nearby timber. As the man felt the smooth, slick finish that had been polished by so many hands over the years, memories came flooding back.

He remembered how, as a young farmer, he had gone to the timber to choose the railing. He had looked for a willow that was tall enough to reach from the top of the stairs to the very bottom step. He had looked for a tree that was straight and free of gnarls. At last, he had found the right one. He took the ax, stripped the branches from the slender trunk and brought it back to his home. When he anchored it into the wall, he even used small willow branches to support the railing.

He remembered how the railing had helped his aged mother travel up and down the stairs each morning to the kitchen and each night to her bedroom. She had never fallen, even when she became so frail. Ninety years, up and down, but no more.

He remembered how the railing had stayed firm when his youngest son would try to slide down the slick surface on the seat of his pants. More than once, that same son had his seat warmed after one of his tricks. He half-smiled to himself as he thought of the times his son had "scared the daylights" out of his sisters in one of his escapades. But no more.

Memories hurt too much tonight, so he closed his mind once again. Ever since this afternoon when the Marine Sergeant had knocked at the door, he felt like an old man. He leaned against the railing for support as he continued his long journey up to bed.

Page County 4-H/ Essex Whirlwinds 4-H Club

By Martin Head

The 4-H group that I worked with was led by a man named Ernie Almquist. I remember Ernie being quite a worker. He was untiring, especially with the kids; I was just the back-up. Our job was to go around and look at kids' projects and give them advice. The kids we worked with showed either pigs or calves.

For my children, when it came time to sell the pigs, it always seemed that Vivian, my daughter, would get more for her pig than Bob, my son. So, Bob would always have Vivian take his pig in; it seemed to be this way probably because Vivian had her pig's toenails polished, and she was also better looking than Bob.

One year at the county fair, a big rain storm came and the people with cattle rushed to the fair to save their cattle, because they were only in tents. All of the cattle were okay once we got there, but it was quite a scare.

I don't remember much these days; this is just about all I know. My mind is so fuzzy, probably because I'm almost 99 years old. I'm sorry I can't add more for your book, but Father Time has taken his toll on me.

Editor's note: Martin Head recently celebrated his 100th birthday. He shared the above story with his great-granddaughter Emily.

4-H Reminiscences

By Florence Green Hoffmann

My name is Florence Green Hoffmann. I grew up in Page County in Fremont Township in the 1920s and 1930s. Our farm was 14 miles northwest of Clarinda, 13 miles northeast of Shenandoah, and 15 miles south of Red Oak. We were on a rural mail route out of Essex, 7 miles away. One-room, rural schools dotted the countryside, 2 miles apart. My school, grades 1 through 8, was Maple Hill, which had also been attended by my father, Edward Green. Goldenrod School, now a part of the Nodaway Valley Museum in Clarinda, was a mile south and 2 miles west of our farm. Almost everyone in our community came from a Swedish immigrant heritage. Social life was centered in church–Fremont Lutheran Church at Nyman, the Mission Covenant Church and Bethesda Lutheran Church.

We had busy, full, happy lives, but we were living with mud roads, snowdrifts and outdoor toilets. Rural electrification didn't come until the '40s. Paved and graveled roads, now everywhere,

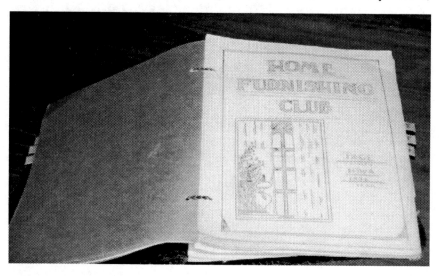

came gradually. The '20s and '30s were difficult years for farmers–drought, grasshoppers, chinch bugs and the low crop prices of the Great Depression. Times were tough for farmers long before the '29 stock market crash.

We were part of a strong homogeneous community, but we were rural isolates. When we went off to high school–Essex, Coburg, Red Oak–we were the "country kids," not readily accepted at first by the "city kids."

This is background to explain how 4-H came to be an important part of my early years. Everything in the program seemed to open up a promising new world–just what Jessie Field had in mind, I think.

Excellent materials were provided for all the clubs by home economists of the Extension Service operating out of Iowa State University. We had two years of clothing, two years of nutrition (bread baking and canning), two years of home furnishings and two years of home efficiency. Seventy years later, I still have a piece of furniture I refinished as a 4-H club project. In addition, we were exposed to health standards, art appreciation, music appreciation, drama, conservation and the idea of intercultural exchanges. There was a world beyond southwestern Iowa.

The Fremont Farmerettes were organized in 1930 with Mrs. Melvin Lefgren as our leader. She was a farm wife with much artistic ability and get-up-and-go spirit. Soon, there came to our community a new minister, whose wife, Mrs. W. Albert Ericson, had studied home economics at Bethany College in Lindsborg, Kansas. She became our leader in 1932.

There were many opportunities to develop leadership skills. It was my good fortune to be president of our local club for three years, Page County president for a year and state historian for a year. Three state conventions at Ames, a trip to the National 4-H Club Congress in Chicago (which I won for my five-year record book), and a trip to the Iowa State Fair representing Page County on a demonstration team were very special experiences. Our demonstration team subject was "the uses of canned tomato juice." We all had fun and made new friends. Remember, we were teenagers. Responsibilites, challenges, competition, opportunities for service, appreciation of the organization and scope of 4-H club work all were part of the experience. In 1936, I wrote for my record book an essay on "Living 4-H, a Story of What Club Work Has Meant to Me." Here is an excerpt:

> *To me, 4-H has always been an inspiration and a challenge. I remember the thrill of my first trip to convention. The music, the talks, the recreation, the very atmosphere and spirit of "living 4-H"–everything seemed very wonderful to me. I went home full of many new hopes and visions and with the resolution that I must try my best to impart some of that inspiration to the folks at home. Each succeeding convention and state fair, and last year, the National 4-H Club Congress, has meant renewed zeal and renewed determination to "make the best better." These, of course, were high points during the year. 4-H club work in itself has meant a challenge to live up to our uniform, to the ideals which it symbolizes. 4-H has encouraged a desire to live valiantly, to think and do and be my best. It has meant inspirations, visions, and broadening horizons–yes, living 4-H has truly been an adventure!*

I was only 17 when I wrote that and pretty idealistic; 65 years later, I still have warm, fuzzy feelings about 4-H clubs. My active participation ended, however, when I went off to the University of Iowa in 1937. There, I pursued a course of study in history and education, met a handsome law student whom I married in 1940 and moved to Des Moines. For some time, I kept in touch with other state officers and attended reunions on the Iowa State campus. I attended the Iowa State Fair and always visited the 4-H Building to see the exhibits and a demonstration or two. Through the decades, there were noticeable changes. Prosperity and technology meant lifestyle changes. Upscale furniture replaced dressing tables made of orange crates. Food preservation looked more to freezing than to canning. New programs were introduced; particularly handsome were the photography exhibits. The 4-H clubs were expanded to include urban members and urban ideas. All of these changes, keeping pace with what was happening in the 20th century, I applaud. Positive progress in the 21st century is surely a given.

The 4-H club friends with whom I am still in touch today are my demonstration team partner, Cleone Lungren Nelson of Stanton, and Ruth Ericson, the 1934 Page County health champion, now a psychiatrist in Dallas, Texas. We three enjoyed our first State Fair together, a few State Fairs since and a whole series of get-togethers that we plan for ourselves every two or three years. In 1998, the year all three of us turned 80, we took a driving trip together through the Sandhills of Nebraska. In 2000, we took a driving trip up and down the Mississippi River Road to Wisconsin. All three of us have visited the Nodaway Valley Museum together. We have other bonds – church, school, family friendships, Swedish heritage – but all three of us often mention our 4-H good times.

Farm-related Careers

From the Farm to Congress and the Courtroom

By Nancy Thompson

It didn't occur to me, growing up on a farm in southern Iowa, that I would spend my career defending and working with family farmers. I loved the farm, but it didn't cross my mind at the time that there was any reason for farmers to need a lawyer (which I had decided in eighth grade to become). If I had known then that I would spend decades trying to help family farmers stay in farming and help beginning farmers get a start, I probably would have paid closer attention to some things. For instance, I would have thought more about why my father, who was a full-time farmer, also had to have a full-time career off the farm. I would have asked more questions about why farmers who planted the southern Iowa hillsides with beans and corn got more money from the government than my father did for keeping the hillsides in hay so the soil wouldn't erode. I would have asked Dad to explain why he was a member of a farm group and voted for politicians that did nothing to help family farmers.

Timing is likely what led me to spend my career among farmers. I graduated from the University of Iowa College of Law in 1984 at the height of the "farm crisis," which probably meant there were more job opportunities available in farm law then than at any other time before or since. When I entered law school, I didn't expect to focus my legal career on farmers, but by the time I was leaving, I was sure I would like working with farmers more than with a firm full of lawyers. So, I took a job in a tiny town in Nebraska as the Legal Aid Society's Farm Law Attorney and as an attorney for the Center for Rural Affairs. I worked on farm credit, aid for beginning farmers, corporate farming and economic development issues. I suddenly found myself on the front lines, responding to farmers facing foreclosure, to the FDIC closing rural banks and to new laws intended to help farmers restructure debt. It was a great time to become a farm lawyer, and it led to great opportunities to be an advocate for beginning and other family farmers in Congress, state legislatures, courtrooms and elsewhere.

In 1984, I started asking the questions I should have asked growing up on the farm, but I don't think I am any closer to finding the answers today. I'm still baffled by why more farmers and farm groups don't advocate for tough commodity payment limitations and anti-corporate farming laws that would help put farming back into the hands of families who will provide a majority of a farm's labor and management. Scores of studies have proven that smaller, family farms are better for the economy of rural communities, but farm policy doesn't reflect that fact. I still wonder why we can't more adequately tie federal assistance to a farmer's commitment to the environment. The new Conservation Security Program is finally the kind of support that environmentally-concerned farmers deserve. Yet the program struggles for funding, so huge farms keep getting hundreds of thousands of dollars from taxpayers in return for only a minimal commitment to soil and water quality.

I'm still amazed at how many people think industrialization in livestock production is the result of some economic "invisible hand" that leads to an inevitable decline in smaller, independent livestock producers. Warped farm policies, not inevitable economics, lead to industrialization, and those policies can be reversed to promote new opportunities in small scale farm production. I still don't understand why it's easy to give lip service to the needs of beginning farmers, but it's apparently hard to adopt bold credit, estate and tax laws that actually will lead to more of them in our rural communities.

I still work with family farmers, and I'm still learning–maybe I can find the answers to my questions before it's too late. I should have asked these questions earlier, but I was having too much fun on the farm.

Nancy Thompson practices law in Des Moines, Iowa, but dreams of being a farmer one day.

Early Biological Warfare or How the Transition from Muscle Power to Machine Power Got a Boost

By Jim Boyt

My father, J. Walter Boyt, was president of the Boyt Harness Company, a Des Moines harness manufacturer for workhorses, selling basically to the upper Midwest or "snow belt."

Early tractors, with their steel wheels and lugs, had largely failed in the heavy Midwestern soils by the mid 1930s. I remember my dad speaking of seeing them standing idle at many farmsteads because they were useless under any but the best conditions. Thus, though the early tractors made a dent in the workhorse harness business, this largely disappeared by the 1930s.

My father was a regular lecturer at what was then Iowa State College. He would explain the advantages of farming with horses. In that time of extreme cash scarcity, the farmer raised his own fuel and, of course, much of the time the horses ate grass or other plant life that had no economic value. A side benefit was a regular supply of colts, which could be sold.

However, the trend toward larger farms had begun and many farmers wanted more power than they could get from a team of two, three or even four horses. Someone had invented the "multiple hitch," which permitted efficient hitches of five or more horses to be driven with a single pair of lines.

These hitches required specially-engineered "eveners" that would even the load on the horses as they worked. The Boyt Harness Company had these made in quantity and sold them throughout its distribution territory. They greatly increased the ease and efficiency of larger hitches.

But about that time, the upper Midwest was hit with a plague of equine encephalitis or horse sleeping sickness; just maddening to the farmers. The horses didn't die; they just stood there and could do no work.

My brother, sister and I, grade-schoolers at the time, were hired to put out the company's mailing on a piece-work basis instead of getting an allowance. We folded the company literature when needed, assembled whatever pieces were to be mailed and stuffed the envelopes, keeping them segregated by states. That was all the post office required for bulk mailing back then.

When the plague of sleeping sickness hit, one of the items in every mailing to the harness dealers was veterinary information on how farmers could alleviate, at least to some extent, sleeping sickness in their areas.

By then, rubber-tired tractors were becoming more common. They had two great advantages: they would work under most field conditions, and they did not get sick. And, unlike the horses, you could turn them off when you were not using them.

The end of World War II was the beginning of the end for workhorses for commercial agriculture in the upper Midwest.

Many farmers kept a team around to do certain special jobs such as weed mowing and manure spreading in the spring and, it appears, partly for sentimental reasons. Anyone who has spread manure with a team of horses going downwind remembers it as quite an experience. Both you and the team were pelted with manure; you didn't like it and neither did the team.

Before long, horse-killing packing plants sprang up to make dog food out of the big workhorses that were no longer needed on the farm.

The old-time harness dealers went out of business and, to their dying days, they insisted the sleeping sickness virus or germ or whatever it was, had been spread by the people selling tractors and gasoline.

John Wesley LaGrange: Horse and Buggy Doctor, Marion, Iowa, 1878-1923

By W.S. LaGrange

D r. J.W. LaGrange was born in Franklin, Indiana in 1849. He was one of nine children, including five boys, three of whom became medical doctors and two druggists. John Wesley graduated from Hanover College in Indiana and obtained his medical degree from Rush Medical College in Chicago (Rush Presbyterian Hospital in Chicago) in 1877. He practiced one year in Vinton and moved to Marion in 1879, where he was a family physician for 40 years. In 1923, he retired and moved to Florida where he died in 1925.

John Wesley's son was William F. LaGrange, professor of Animal Science at Iowa State University from 1920 to 1965. Since John Wesley died in 1925, and I was born in 1931, I did

not know my grandfather, but I did hear stories about him from my father.

Dr. LaGrange had his medical office near downtown Marion close to the Methodist Church. He and his family lived just one block away. Their home included a barn that housed the horses that the doctor used to reach his patients in town and in the surrounding countryside. I have pictures of him both astride a horse and in a buggy. My father said Dr. LaGrange bought and used retired trotting horses to get around in his practice. He always kept at least two horses in his barn. My father recalls that his father sometimes would be gone all night on a call to visit a sick patient or to help a mother deliver her baby. Winter weather posed a challenge for making house calls and contributed to some overnight absences from home.

In my family picture album, there is one of my father standing beside a very young colt as well as one with him in a buggy that Dr. LaGrange used in his medical practice. My father told me once that, as a young boy, he was driving a horse and buggy when the horse got spooked and started to run away. This resulted in my father's leg being broken as his leg hit a telephone pole.

According to the obituary published in the Marion newspaper dated February 12, 1925, Dr. LaGrange served as County Physician (presumably Linn County), Commissioner of Insanity, Board of Health Chairman, Railroad Physician, and Examiner for Insurance for the U.S. Pension Board. It said, "he was the ideal of the old family doctor of early days; when prayer and physic were interchangeable, and the physician was also a counselor, intimate family friend and spiritual adviser. He was a dispenser of medicine, 'tis true', but a dispeller equally of morbid and unhealthy mental and spiritual disorders, and a living incentive to gladness and goodness."

Editor's note: Prepared by W.S. LaGrange, grandson of Dr. J.W. LaGrange, Iowa State University

Birth in a Chicken House

By James Lucas

The veterinary profession, especially in general mixed country practice, lends itself to a lot of experiences that only a veterinarian could imagine.

Many times, the clients are naive about their pet. "Oh, my dog won't bite" or "my horse won't kick;" that is about the time the animal unloads on you.

A favorite quote of mine is from a phone call I received one night at 2:00 am, "Gosh, Doc, I hope I didn't wake you." Or, "Were you in bed, Doc?" Or, "I tried to get the other vet, but he wouldn't answer his phone." I would like to have answered with this, "What the heck are most people doing this time of night?" In the end, it's just part of being a veterinarian.

February nights in Iowa can be breathtaking. Temperatures around zero can equate to 50 below with wind chill. It was just such a night when the phone rang at 1:30 in the morning. A voice on the other end slowly asked, "Were you sleeping Jim?"

I immediately recognized the voice of Jim Wells, a Good Samaritan bachelor. I wanted to answer "No Jim, I was up canning tomatoes." Remembering Jim as being a good caretaker of his livestock, I was my usual easy-going self, considering what time it was.

"I have a cow that has been calving since 6 p.m. She isn't gaining, so I figured it's about time to check her out," Jim told me over the phone. Jim also added, "I tried the other vet in Parnell so as not to bother you, but he said that he doesn't do night calls anymore; I thought maybe you would help my cow."

I thought to myself, that's nice to know that I could have done this in the early evening since the cow's been laboring since 6 p.m. I was even happier knowing I was second choice, but at least Jim was honest with me. I told him that I'd be right over. I ambled into my coveralls and boots and headed out on my way to Missouri.

Jim and I met in the driveway, where he informed me that the cow was penned in the old non-electrified chicken house; he hoped that I had a flashlight. Jim remarked, "She was real tame when I drove her in, but now she seems a little nervous."

"Oh, boy" I said, "this sounds like fun."

I stuck my head in the door of the dingy little chicken house; it was a 1900s version of a hen egg-laying house, where rows of unused nests lined the wall. I looked around for a pole to tie a rope to, but couldn't find one. I couldn't see any avenue of escape either, except for a small feed room. For my own protection, I always looked for an escape route in case all hell broke loose.

The cow warily looked at me, but did not offer to charge. I walked in with my equipment; I had a flashlight, a lariat rope and an obstetrics bag containing a chain, a snare, a bucket of warm water and a calf jack. The calf jack is a tool about 6 feet long, which helps deliver hard-to-pull calves.

I got a rope around the cow's head on the first throw; amazingly, she didn't react wildly. I was able to thread the rope through a hole around a support of the building. I was positive that would restrain her. We had her tied short so I could begin my examination.

The calf was normal in presentation, but the cow's pelvis was extremely small. Under the conditions, I feared doing a cesarean, so I went ahead and attempted delivery. I placed the OB chains on the calf's feet and pulled. Its head went back, so

I put a head snare on and again applied pressure. There didn't seem to be birthing room, so I put the calf jack in place and attached it to the chain and snare. As I tightened the pressure, the cow became hysterical and lunged and jumped. All of a sudden, the restraint rope released, and the cow was loose. My 6-foot jack was firmly in place, sticking out of her like a club. I yelled to Jim to get to safety as the 1,500 pound animal was bucking through the dark building. As the cow banged around, the calf jack sounded like a gun firing every time it hit the floor. The swinging jack could have easily killed one of us.

The more the jack banged, the wilder the cow became. For safety, I dove into the dark feed room and shut the door; Jim had gotten outside. Finally, the cow tired and began to settle down. Not venturing far from my safe hole, I carefully retrieved my rope. I looped her again and retied her to the support; thankfully, she didn't offer any resistance. The unborn calf was surprisingly still alive, and with one more hard pull, the calf came through the pelvis.

A miracle had happened yet again. A new, vibrant, live calf flopped back and forth in that dark, dingy henhouse. It was trying to get on its feet but kept falling back down on its side. We released the cow, and her maternal instinct kicked in as she aggressively began licking the newborn. She paid absolutely no attention to Jim or I.

"Isn't that something," Jim said. "It was a little trouble, but it was worth it."

"Yes," I replied, "it's always so great to get a live calf."

We bade our good-byes when I realized that I was wide awake. I took a deep breath of the fresh, cold air and saw that the stars were bright. There was a big, beautiful full moon overhead. There was no wind, and I felt a bead of sweat trickle down my neck.

As I drove down that old Missouri road, I crossed a wooden bridge that had no rails. The frost on the roadside weeds flashed on and off like Christmas lights, reflecting in my truck's headlights. What a beautiful sight! I thought how most people were sleeping in the warmth of their beds, unaware of just what they were missing. Just then, I thought to myself, I love being a veterinarian.

The Life Story of a County Seat Town Super Market

Carlson's Super Valu (1960 – 1993)

By Carl A. Carlson, Owner/Operator

With my college business degree completed, military obligation fulfilled and some retailing experience with Firestone, I returned to my hometown, Greenfield, to join my father (Marion Carlson) in business at the Maid-Rite Café. Our plan was to combine the café, at the main intersection of the two state highways coming into town, with a new business. The winds of change were evident for the grocery business in most county seat towns in southern Iowa. Storefront, neighborhood groceries and country stores were being replaced with small supermarkets. Dad and I saw potential for a new supermarket next to the Maid-Rite.

We opened Carlson's Super Valu on November 10, 1960. It was an integral part of Greenfield's retail sector for the next 33 years.

Our business plan was to establish a ground-up supermarket. The Adair County Bank loaned 12 percent of the start-up financing. Our friend, Frank Maynes, bought the lots west of the café and built a 4,000-square-foot cement block building, which we leased. Super Valu, Inc. extended us credit for the fixtures and start-up inventory.

The selection of a Super Valu, Inc. franchise proved to be excellent. They were our wholesaler through all 33 years.

Super Valu, Inc. could pass on the savings of mass buying from food processors and handlers. Their full-service, independent retailer support mission provided us payroll and accounting services, expert advice, engineering services, cost breaks on equipment and fixtures, help to bring in technological advances and more.

The first five years were a much tougher struggle than we'd anticipated. We worked long hours, while being very visible in community affairs to build good will. We spent sparsely; "put our best foot forward;" advertised extensively; kept our prices low compared to other retailers; and used many games and gimmicks to boost sales. We gave Gold Bond trading stamps for every sale. Dad made many trips to Des Moines to pick up Gold Bond redemption merchandise for our customers.

The selection of items we stocked was rural in nature–bedding plants, bulk seed potatoes, garden seeds, barrel bulk vinegar, chicken grit, block lick salt for cattle and much more. In the early years, we bought dressed hens directly from farm wives.

Finally, we gambled on Bank Roll as a customer incentive program. It worked! Our repeat business was improved, and the customers liked the fun of this game of chance. Our sales grew, and we quit losing money each month for the first time.

The store was open from 8 a.m. to 8 p.m. Monday through Saturday. Later, we were open seven days each week for longer hours.

By the early 1970s, the building was far too small. On Saturdays, customers stood in line the full length of the store to check out.

In April 1975, we moved into the newly constructed, free-span metal building on Iowa State Highway 25. The new building had 9,200 square feet of space. An on-premise bakery was our new venture, and a dock made it possible for us to unload pallets of groceries from the warehouse. The parking lot was bigger and was twice expanded. In two stages, we enlarged the building to about 15,000 square feet without overloading ourselves with unmanageable debt. Heavy debt loads challenged many businesses in Greenfield during the

1980s. We added a deli with catering service and expanded our merchandise quantity and variety.

We improved our traditions of being a fun place to shop and customer friendly. We sold lottery tickets and participated in the can and bottle recycling program. With tech support from Super Valu, we installed new technologies, such as scanning, ordering with phone hook-ups, computers, satellite connections to the warehouse and more. An affordable and attractive pricing structure was our continuing goal. My wife and I, our two children and many of our full-time employees were very active in community affairs. For a few years, we extended our business hours to 24 hours a day, seven days a week. We never quit extending credit to customers in special need.

Our employees were so important. Many of our best employees found a "new life" in the store when hitting a personal cross-roads. Super Valu, Inc. helped us with excellent on-the-job training. Many teens and young adults started worthy careers in our store as they learned transferable skills for success. We attempted to be responsive to the personal needs of all our employees and celebrated with them the special events in their lives. Good humor abounded.

Our constant endeavor was to be supportive of community activities by participating and making many financial contributions. We entered reclaimed old cars, floats and other things in Greenfield's and other parades. Many youth and women's organizations raised funds at Saturday morning bake sales held at our store. The local units of farm commodity organizations held promotional activities in conjunction with our meat department.

In 1988, the business didn't post an increase in gross sales for the first time. We endeavored to keep a positive attitude and continued to have fun with our work. Whining has no place in a well-run supermarket.

According to the U.S. Census of Population reports, there were 10,893 people living in Adair County in 1960. By the time we sold the business in 1993, the number had declined to 8,409. The new mass merchandisers were taking business from our trade area. In the late '80s, the number of births per year fell below the number of deaths for the county. That is about the same time our sales growth began to sag.

In 1992, the economic development organization and the city council community extended Fareway, Inc. TIF (Tax Increment Financing) to open a chain store of a new prototype on the site of the recently closed high school. Place's, a small general merchandizing chain, received public subsidies to move to a new store building next to Fareway. It was obvious our store was oversized for our shrinking market. Our business projections were discouraging.

In January 1993, we sold the business to our wholesaler, Super Valu, Inc., which operated the store 20 months before liquidating the inventory and auctioning the fixtures. We sold the building to Greenfield Lumber Company for less than 30 percent of the assessed valuation. Our son had expected to come back to Greenfield to manage our store after getting training and experience. Instead, he's been part of store management teams in four states in 10 years at Wal-Mart Supercenters.

Let's Keep the 'I' in Iowa

By LaVon Griffieon

I was 2 when my mom went to work in town. She wasn't seeking personal fulfillment or furthering her career, she was working as a waitress so our family could pay the bills. My dad and I were left at home on our 160-acre, rented farm while my older brother and sister went off to grade school.

In the 1950s men didn't baby sit or do childcare, so I assumed the role of Dad's right-hand man, never minding the fact that I was a girl.

The four years I spent at home with Dad, before the public school system interrupted my education, are still my most treasured years. We ran trap lines, hunted and fished. I grew up in the seat of a John Deere A, and I loved it. We milked cows and had baby bottle lambs to feed. I never had a clue we were poor, because the time I spent with Dad made my life rich. Dad planted seeds in my heart and mind that wouldn't germinate until decades later.

I grew up in an Iowa with bustling small-town main streets and tree-lined, residential neighborhoods. In these towns and neighborhoods, kids were free to ride their bikes or pull together a sandlot ballgame without an adult to guide them. When I hear about the young, educated minds that flee our state today, I have to question, "What went wrong? Why is Iowa no longer a place where young people want to stay?"

My 21-year-old daughter and 18-year-old son are knowledgeable on this subject. They claim to have been told by teachers their entire academic life that if you want to be a success or have a six-figure salary, you'll have to leave Iowa. My kids question the need to chase after a six-figure salary. They look at our family, our farm and how we live, and they like it. They have decided they want to be a part of the century-old legacy we call home. They've also been told they can't make a living farming. It appears, however, they are preparing to challenge that idea.

Most Iowans think of farming as big tractors, corn and soybeans. That is how our family currently makes its living. However, I think my children are choosing a different path. At 13, my son, Nick, wanted a four-wheeler. My husband and I really weren't interested in him having a four-wheeler. Our response was, "Fine. You earn the money, and you can buy the four-wheeler."

Nick decided to make his fortune raising broiler-chickens. He ordered 100 chicks, bought the feed, paid the locker to butcher them and ended up losing $13. Not easily discouraged, he decided to rethink his enterprise. He discovered that feed was his largest expense. He bought corn from his dad, borrowed the neighbor's grinder-mixer, got an antibiotic and hormone-free pre-mix from a local elevator and made his own feed. By having his feed "antibiotic-free, no hormones added" he added value to his product and could sell the chickens for a higher price. He has continued to make money over the past six years with his broiler business and has expanded into heritage turkeys and natural egg sales.

The location of our farm between Des Moines and Ames puts our family in a perfect position to capitalize on local food sales. Consumers have become more concerned about food safety since the BSE scare and are increasingly health conscious with education from obesity studies and 5-a-Day programs. Local food security is another consideration. Iowa, which touts itself as the "Food Capital of the World," imports 86 percent of its food from outside the state. The average food item travels 1,200-1,800 miles to arrive on the grocery shelf. There is a three-day supply of food in our local grocery warehouses. If that supply was cut off through a transportation catastrophe, the chaotic scene at grocery stores would resemble what we normally experience only before a blizzard. There is a 40-day supply of food in the world. That's thought of as a surplus. There is a 240-year supply of proven oil reserves in the ground at current usage rates. That's thought of as a shortage. I believe that a good, wholesome supply of local food is necessary near all towns and cities and should not be considered simply as a niche market near a metropolitan area.

Our family recently took a class at Drake called "Growing Your Small Market Farm." We learned about writing a business plan and current trends. We learned that each resident of Polk County eats 66 pounds of beef annually, which caught our attention as beef producers. Polk County's population is 374,601 and county residents eat 61 percent of their meals at home. That means a market potential of 15,130,884 pounds of beef. If our family could capture even a small percentage of that market, my kids could easily make a living staying right here in Polk County.

As for the future for the rest of Iowa agriculture, I see a bright light. Many small communities in Iowa are finding themselves with fewer services and sources of income. For many, the Casey's store has become the equivalent of a grocery store. Some Casey's stores in Iowa are franchises and allow the sale of locally grown products. Most convenience stores are not a major source for healthy eating, however. If farmers had a local outlet to sell their produce, money could be kept within the state. Other markets would be schools, nursing homes and state facilities, such as colleges, prisons, hospitals and the State Capitol food services.

Iowa had 215,000 farms in 1940. Farm numbers are fewer than 91,000 today. In 1929, Iowa produced 52,915 acres of vegetables, while today, Iowa produces 12,495 acres. Warren County used to be the apple capital of the world; today, we have only 2,616 acres of orchards in the entire state of Iowa compared to 63,185 in 1929. If we would create markets for local foods, producers would respond. Surprisingly, many of my kids' college-aged friends would like to farm. Growing food would offer another way for young people to enter farming without the huge financial debt load for machinery and land needed to farm with conventional methods. Two acres of vegetables are about all one farmer can handle, yet it is enough to make a living for a family if a market is available.

Iowans spend $8 billion a year on food. Economic multiplier principles state that dollars spent locally multiply seven times.

If even half of that food was raised within Iowa and sold locally, Iowa's economic crisis could be a thing of the past.

Iowa needs to look at its resources: prime world-class soils, frequent rainfalls and an abundance of fresh water. It has 950 cities; more than any state besides Texas. If you grew up on a farm or in a small town, odds are that is where your family and those people who care about you live. It is the lifestyle that many people on both the East and West coasts long for. It is what suburban subdivisions try to replicate with New Urbanist design techniques. But why replicate it, when you can experience the real thing? Let's have Iowa's economic development dollars start working to make small-town Iowa more appealing to our college graduates. Let's work to make rural Iowa economically viable, environmentally sound, health-promoting in body and soul and locally owned. Let's allow the next generation of Iowans to grow up working side by side with their parents on small farms and in local businesses, like I was able to do.

About the Farm Business Association Foundation...

The Farm Business Association Foundation (FBAF) was established on the belief that there are opportunities in agriculture, although the nature and form of opportunities may have changed over time.

The Foundation, through philanthropy, works to develop and support new tools and programs for present and future generations of agricultural producers and rural communities.

GOALS

- To enhance the business skills of Iowa's farm families.
- To help rural citizens achieve their personal and family goals.
- To aid in the economic and social survival of the rural community.
- To be an educator and facilitator.

If you would like to learn more about the Foundation, please contact:

Farm Business Association Foundation
226 SE 16th Street
Ames, Iowa 50010
Phone: (515) 233-5802
www.iowafarmbusiness.org

ISBN 1-41204350-6